# FUNDAMENTAL
# THOUGHTS IN
# ECONOMICS

**KENNIKAT PRESS SCHOLARLY REPRINTS**

Dr. Ralph Adams Brown, Senior Editor

Series on
**ECONOMIC THOUGHT, HISTORY AND CHALLENGE**
Under the General Editorial Supervision of
Dr. Sanford D. Gordon
*Professor of Economics, State University of New York*

# FUNDAMENTAL THOUGHTS IN ECONOMICS

*By* GUSTAV CASSEL

KENNIKAT PRESS
Port Washington, N. Y./London

FUNDAMENTAL THOUGHTS IN ECONOMICS

First published in 1925
Reissued in 1971 by Kennikat Press
Library of Congress Catalog Card No: 71-137933
ISBN 0-8046-1438-5

Manufactured by Taylor Publishing Company    Dallas, Texas

KENNIKAT SERIES ON ECONOMIC THOUGHT
HISTORY AND CHALLENGE

## PREFACE

ONE often feels that when a scientist has written a long series of papers and books which may have been published in different languages and different countries, it would be a very useful thing to have a short summary of his works, giving prominence to the fundamental thoughts which form their common basis or unite them into a coherent whole. For my own part, I have long been aware that it was my duty thus to expound the leading ideas in my economic works. The present book is an endeavour to fulfil this obligation. My immediate inducement to write it was an invitation from the University of London to give a series of lectures on Advanced Economics, and I here print these lectures as they were written for the purpose.

It is in the very nature of this book that its subject should embrace the greater part of those economic problems which are of essential importance either for economic theory or for practical economic policy. I hope that the book as it stands will prove to be of real use to any one desirous of penetrating to a deeper understanding of these problems, and I also venture to hope that, in order to get a more comprehensive idea of the subjects it treats of, readers of this book may be induced hereby to extend their studies to my main works. I have therefore added footnotes giving references to them.

GUSTAV CASSEL.

LONDON,
*June* 1925.

# CONTENTS

# FUNDAMENTAL THOUGHTS IN
## ECONOMICS

# CHAPTER I

## AIMS AND METHODS OF ECONOMIC THEORY

WHEN I received the great honour of being invited to give some lectures on advanced economics in the University of London, I naturally felt that it was expected of me that I should expound something that occupied a central position in my work. But the most central is obviously the elementary principles underlying the whole work, the ideas which run through the various investigations and make a logical unit of them. So I decided to try to give here an exposition of the leading thoughts which have guided me in my economic investigations and bound them together into a coherent economic system.

Of course, I did not begin my scientific work by conceiving a ready-made system from which every truth could be deduced and into which the reality had at any price to be pressed in order to fit. This is no truly scientific way of going to work. If, as I think, my different investigations form a unity which in some sense can be called an economic system, although by no means complete, it is because I have tried at every step to let my aims and methods be determined solely by the essential *economic* nature of the subject to be investigated. If we consistently observe this rule I think we should find that, in economic theory, there is not so much room for arbitrary decisions as has generally been believed. In fact, there is much of necessity in economic life and also much of necessity in the ways of analysing this life. The important thing is just to find out these necessities. If we try to do this, and if we keep our attention constantly directed upon what is, from a purely economic point of view, essential in the matter we have to investigate, our results will prove to possess a natural coherency and logical unity.

Today I intend to give, from this leading point of view, a short exposition of the aims and methods of economic theory, as I view them.

The first question which economic science has to clear up is the question of the justification of its own existence. The object of the science is the economic life. It is then very natural to ask whether those people, who live in the midst of this economic life and are working practically with its problems, should not know it better than people who stand aside and look on and are only able to get a second-hand knowledge of real economic events. Leaders of industry, trade and banking do in fact often know more of what is really going on in their respective fields than most representatives of the economic science. In this respect science is inevitably handicapped. If, therefore, economic science has any justification for its existence, it must be because it has its own aims which are neglected by practical people, but which have nevertheless essential importance and necessity. This is in fact the case, and a closer analysis of the difference between a scientific and a practical view of economic life is very useful for the science itself when it wishes to acquire a conscious and clear idea of its own peculiar functions.

First of all, science must always, in discussing causes and effects, take the *whole complex* as its object. It cannot stop at any arbitrarily chosen link in the chain. It must consider the totality of occurrences which are in economic reality inextricably connected with one another. For the business man, it is in most cases sufficient if he is able to form a correct judgment of the very nearest consequences of his acts. If he tried to think further, he would perhaps lose time, and even the concentration of will, to act. To him also his own business has an importance which makes it for him the central point of economic life. For science such a view is impossible. Science must look upon economic life as a whole, and consequences which from the point of view of the individual business man are remote, may from a scientific standpoint have at least the same importance, as nearer ones.

The practical consequence for economic science is that, in principle, it must always take an entire economic unit as its object. This means that economic science must always assume the economy which it wishes to analyse, as being enclosed within itself and having no connections with an outside world. For if any such connections should exist, it would be necessary, in order to get a complete view of the totality of the chains of causes and effects, to take even these connections into consideration, i.e., to widen the object of the investigation and regard a greater, but in itself complete economic unit. The unit chosen may be a small one, e.g., an isolated peasant economy, or a large one, the economy of a modern people or of the whole world. The object must be determined by the character of the investigations, but in any case it is essential that it should be a closed economy.

Such an economy is always a more or less extended social organization, and the object of economic science is therefore always essentially a social phenomenon. In order to accentuate this, it is suitable to designate the object of our science as "social economy." This is also the reason why I have called my main work on this subject *The Theory of Social Economy*.[1]

There is in fact an essential difference between social-economic and private-economic ways of handling economic problems. The difference is indeed so great that a sentence which is quite correct when used in a private-economic sense, may be absolutely false when applied to

---

[1] London, Fisher Unwin, 1923. New York, Harcourt, Brace, 1924.

social economics. E.g., for the individual it is no doubt an advantage to have more money, for a society not. Much that is quite possible from the private-economic point of view will be found impossible when extended to the whole of social economy. The consumption of capital, e.g., seems a simple thing for the individual capitalist, but it is impossible for the society, except in a restrained and entirely different meaning.

Another point in which economic science differs from practical economic thinking is that the science is always directed towards a grasping of the *realities* of economic life, whereas the business man is, in his economic reasonings, mostly satisfied with the external form. This statement would perhaps at first sight appear to be rather daring. One is disposed a priori to believe that the practical man stands nearer to the concrete reality, and that a theorist would be rather inclined to abstract views. However, this is not so in the economic sphere. Modern economic life is in fact so accustomed to express everything in very abstract terms of money that mere figures are looked upon by practical people as the only realities. Incomes are represented as sums of money, and it is felt to be a very strange idea that our real incomes should consist of the goods and services which we consume. A person's wealth is spoken of as so and so much money, and, if he gets richer, he is supposed to possess so and so many units of money more. He has perhaps "made $500,000" in the last year, and then this income is regarded as a sum of money locked up in his safe ready to be expended for any purpose, such as taxes, etc. The cost of the Great War is calculated in figures, and the victorious nations think it desirable and just that they should have indemnities in so and so many milliards. But they find it very queer and disagreeable that they should have to receive a surplus of the former enemies' export goods as payment! Such a way of looking upon things is clearly impossible for a social economic investigation which first of all must make it its object to penetrate the external forms and grasp the realities behind them. This task is not always an easy one. In fact, the way in which the economic scholar is able to master it is to a great extent a decisive factor in the scientific value and the practical usefulness of his work.

Economic science must of course have regard to the money form in which economic realities appear in actual life. The consequence is that in many cases it will prove necessary to give a double description of economic phenomena, first from the point of view of material realities, and secondly from the point of view of the money form in which they usually appear. I have been driven by these considerations to introduce, already in the exposition of the elementary conceptions, a double terminology, such as real capital and real income on the one side, and money capital and money income on the other side, although the last-named terms, better to accord with the usual language of practical life, may be substituted by the simple terms capital and income.

The ways and views of economic science are not only different from those of the business man, but in essential points also from the ideas which usually preponderate in economic policy. The politician in his profession is accustomed to concentrate his whole attention on *power,* and it is therefore for him a very natural idea that everything can be attained on the economic field if only one has sufficient political power at one's disposal. In fact, politicians even believe that they can, simply by using their power, prohibit the logical consequences of their own measures from taking place. This estimation of power is naturally altogether unscientific. Indeed, one of the most important tasks of economic science is to clear up the limitation which is set for the attainable by economic facts and by necessary economic connections. Of course, human will determines the direction and extent of every economic activity, and thereby also in a certain degree the results of the whole economic process. This is indeed the very essence of what we call social economy. It is, however, by no means true that everything flows and that everything can be attained. Fixed limitations exist, and there are hard facts and necessary connections which we are not able arbitrarily to put aside.

A quite naïve overvaluation of political power preponderates in the wide field of speculation on the ideal form of organization and institutions of society. For most people it seems to be a very natural idea that the evils, or more generally the unfavourable occurrences and undesirable facts, of economic life are always the results of fundamental faults in the organization and in the institutions of society. This idea naturally causes people to believe that they could easily bring about almost any improvement if only they possessed sufficient political power for a remodelling of society. This sphere of quite naïve ideas will on closer examination prove to be the ultimate starting-point for every Utopia and for all revolutionary aims. It is therefore very important to examine to what degree different sides of our economic life are dependent or independent of the organization and the institutions of society. Here we have, in fact, one of the most important tasks of economic theory. In order to fulfil this task the theory must, in every one of its investigations, make it clear what extent of validity its results have, whether and in what degree they are independent of the particular form of the society, and, in case they show themselves to be dependent, how they would turn out in other conceivable forms of society. When, e.g., it is said from different sides that the interest on money is not justifiable, and would not exist in a rationally constructed society, it is the function of science to make clear what degree of necessity the phenomenon of interest has or what form it would take under a social order radically different from ours. Such a study would make it clear that the economic necessities have a far greater importance than is imagined by dilettante people absorbed in arbitrary plans for building up a new society. For every earnest student of social conditions it is of course highly important to have recourse to a theory of social economy which, according to the principles here drawn up, is consistently directed towards a study of a complete social economy, of the realities of economic life beneath its monetary form, and of the degree of necessity of its phenomena and its connections. Only such a theory can be a help towards a clear conception of the complex of problems usually denoted as the "social question."

These aims of the theory already give us a valuable general guide with regard to its *methods*. However, the question of methods, and of the principles which ought to govern the choice of methods, requires a closer analysis. We shall find that there is a certain element of necessity even in the choice of methods, and that at least this choice is by no means open to such a complete arbitrariness as has hitherto been preponderant in our science, when almost every writer has believed that he had to make up his own distinctions and his own definitions and find his own ways of handling the problems. Under such conditions occasional points of view have come to play a much greater rôle than they should do, and the consequence has been a deplorable lack of unity, not to say a state of anarchy, in economic science which can easily bring a young student to despair, and which has perhaps no counterpart in any other science of a practical character. The situation would already be much better if people would only observe that *economic* considerations ought to have the deciding influence in the choice of methods in economic science. This would seem a very simple rule, but nevertheless it has very generally been overlooked, and many important discussions on economic science, not to say the whole arrangement of the usual treatises, have often been influenced more by reference to technical and other foreign points of view than to economic ones.

Let us first look at the general ways of procedure which economic science has to choose. Is there anything in the essential nature of the matter which determines these ways? The object of our science is the economy of a certain social unit. The nature of this economy is to some extent influenced by the social order under which it is carried on, but it is also to a certain extent independent of this factor. As I have already said, it is an essential task of economic science to clear up this degree of independence and to show, at each step of its investigations, what is the real validity of its conclusions.

To this end we should make it a rule, in our fundamental investigations, always to introduce a *minimum of assumptions with regard to the organization and the institutions of the society*. Our results will then appear in the full validity which they in fact possess. At the first stage of economic investigations we shall, indeed, make no assumptions at all about the social order. We shall then arrive at conclusions which have a general validity for every social economy without regard to exterior conditions. These conclusions will obviously represent the very core of economic necessities. If we desire further to approach the economic conditions of our own time, it will be necessary to introduce more particular assumptions with regard to the social order. By far the most important of these steps is the assumption of an exchange economy, i.e., a social order where the different households are not generally producing for themselves, but for the whole community, and where they regularly exchange their products or their services for what they need for themselves. A whole series of new phenomena peculiar to this economy will then come into consideration, first of all the phenomena of price and the whole process by which prices are determined. The results of our investigations will, therefore, have a narrower validity. This validity will be still more limited when further assumptions, such as private leadership of industry and private ownership of the means of production, or a system of free competition, are introduced. The important thing is to be careful never to make more assumptions than are necessary with regard to the nature of the investigation in question, so that the validity of our results will at no stage of the investigation be more limited than is necessary. This is important, because, if our results should unnecessarily lose a part of their validity, a part of the truth would also be lost, perhaps just that part which, from some points of view, has the very greatest interest for us.

The observance of this rule enables us to determine the degree to which economic conditions are independent of arbitrary remodellings of social order. In fact, this is the only way by which science can effectively oppose the popular overvaluation of political power. But such a study of social economy is also of great importance for science itself, inasmuch as it is an aid for penetrating deeper into the true nature of important economic phenomena.

It is sometimes useful to form an idea of how certain features of our actual economic life would present themselves in a hypothetical, purely socialistic society, with the whole production centralized in the hands of a single authority, and what modifications the phenomena would thereby undergo. Such an investigation shows that the dogmatic socialists' belief in the radically transforming effect of their social order on the essential economic phenomena is quite groundless, and in fact represents a superstitious overvaluation of political power. At the same time such an investigation is well adapted for throwing new light upon essential sides of our own social economy. For, from certain points of view, the assumed socialistic society may be regarded as the theoretically simplest form of an exchange economy, and the theoretical analysis of such a hypothetical economy may, therefore, be a valuable help towards clearing up real problems of our own actual economy. The same can hardly be said of "Crusoe economics," upon which economic science has bestowed so much flattering attention. For economy, as we know it, is an essentially social process, and economic science has therefore very little to learn from the study of the household of an isolated person.

So much about the assumptions with regard to external conditions. With regard to its own object, economic science has naturally to proceed, as theoretical investigations generally do, from the simplest and therefore the most ab-

stract cases to the more complicated and concrete ones. The way of proceeding is not to
be chosen arbitrarily, but is in the main determined by the essential nature of the reality con-
sidered. In fact, the way of proceeding from
the simple to the complicated is determined as
soon as we know what it is that primarily
makes things complicated in the particular field
of our investigations. Now the main and most
general complication of economic life no doubt
arises from its continual changeability. This
being the case, the successive stages in the procedure from the abstract to the concrete are in
the main already prescribed for economic
theory. At the first stage we must altogether
exclude the changeability, and therefore make
pure *Static Economy* the object of our inquiry.
At the second stage we can introduce such
dynamic conditions as we are able to treat in
a static form, i.e., we have to study *Uniformly
Progressive Economy*. We may call this the
"quasi-static" stage. At the third stage we
come to study what can properly be called
*Economic Dynamics*.

This proceeding, which is a logical consequence of the nature of the object of economic

science, requires at its different stages the use of different methods. At the first and second stages a purely deductive method is obviously necessary. For the assumptions from which we start in these stages are abstract, and in the real world we have no such stages to observe. But as soon as we come to dynamics, the problem assumes a different aspect, for we then have to investigate the deviations which actual life shows from the uniform development which we have studied before. This is clearly possible only by aid of inductive methods which find out these deviations and register them, and which, through a suitable classification of facts, endeavour to clear up the causes of the deviations.

In economic science, the chapter on trade cycles forms the most typical example of an inductive treatment prescribed by the very nature of the matter. In my *Theory of Social Economy* I have naturally in the part of the book concerning trade cycles used purely inductive methods, trying to collect and arrange statistical figures so as to throw a clear light upon the most typical deviations from a uniform development which used to occur in the period from the definite victory of the industrial system to the outbreak of the Great War. Some critics have accused me of this sudden change of methods from the deductive ones which prevail in the former parts of the book where the static and quasi-static stages are treated. But this change is by no means arbitrary. On the contrary, it is necessarily prescribed by the transition from static to dynamic investigations.

The assumptions of static and of uniformly progressive economy have in themselves an element of necessity. This is obvious in the case of static economy. The necessity of an examination of uniformly progressive economy lies in the need for the greatest possible simplification of the idea of a progressive economy. Essential features of economic life, e.g., social accumulation of capital, only exist in a progressive economy, but it is impossible to get a clear idea of them if we do not begin with the assumption of a uniform development. For the further study of purely dynamic conditions it is also necessary to have the uniform development as a standard for a comparison with the fluctuations which take place under actual economic conditions. When we have such a standard these fluctuations take the character of deviations from a normal curve, which represents the uniform development. This observation makes it immediately clear why the examination of a uniform development is absolutely indispensable for every further study of dynamic economy.

But the simplifying assumptions here described are also in the main sufficient, i.e., no other general simplifications are needed. It is therefore unnecessary to introduce other general simplifications, e.g., the usual assumption of a social economy with regular exchange of commodities but without money. Besides, this simplification is not only unnecessary but also quite false. The idea that it would be possible to represent the complications of our actual economy in a simpler form by excluding the element of money has induced economic theory to construct a particular theory of value which is regarded, in the usual type of textbook, as a preliminary to the theory of prices. I intend to show in the course of these lectures not only that this way of proceeding is unnecessary and therefore a waste of time, but also that it is essentially a mistake, because a theory of value in quantitative terms is always and necessarily a theory of prices which presupposes implicitly the existence of money, at least as a unit of account.

An essential feature of economic life is that it is always continued and therefore knows neither beginning nor end. Economic science must consequently take for its object a *perpetual economy,* and particularly a perpetual process of production. This observation has a deciding influence on the conception of the most important and central problems of economic theory as well as on the ways to be chosen for the investigation of these problems. Earlier methods, according to which the production of a commodity was simply followed from the beginning to the end, were modelled according to technical and not to economic views. For such a study many of the most essential features of economic life were fundamentally impossible to understand. This holds true first of all for the processes of saving and of forming concrete capital which can be grasped as social-economic, and perpetual processes only when they are looked upon as features of an always continued

31

social economy. In the light of this view saving loses its old meaning of a storing up of goods which afterwards have to be consumed. What is saved in the continual economy is never produced. Saving then only means a liberating of factors of production which become free to be used for construction of more real capital. Thus the possibility of this construction as a continual process immediately receives its true explanation.

The consideration of continual economy also throws a new light upon the theory of interest. It makes it possible to conceive interest on capital, not as a factor of an isolated business transaction which has its beginning and end, or as an "agio paid in the exchange between future and present goods," but as a regulator of the continual social economy standing in the closest connection with the rate of progress of that economy, and serving both to maintain a certain degree of saving and to limit the demand for the available savings.

In all these examples it is clearly shown how fertile the principle is that we should always make a complete social economy the subject of our investigations. Indeed, the necessity for examining a continual economy is only a consequence of this general principle. For social economy has a continued existence, and does not share the temporary character of the particular transactions carried on within its frame.

Combining these principles of investigation with the principle of proceeding from the static stage to the quasi-static stage of the uniform development, and finally to the dynamic stage, we arrive at an arrangement of the whole investigation, proceeding from the continual static economy, where everything remains unaltered and where we have the best opportunity of defining in the simplest way the most fundamental conceptions of economic theory, and going on to the continual economy with uniform development, where in particular the new conceptions of saving and accumulation of capital come in and can be studied as absolutely constant phenomena. After having gone through these stages, we are well prepared for a study of the dynamic stage, where we likewise study the continual economy. Indeed, the whole problem of trade cycles can and should be studied as the problem of certain fluctuations in the growth of a continual economy and in the internal relations of this economy.

I have not been able to give here more than brief hints as to the way of proceeding. But I hope to have made it clear hereby of what fundamental importance it is for economic theory to choose its methods, not arbitrarily and under the influence of casual points of view, but consciously and with close observance of the essentials of economic life itself and of the requirements which these essentials necessarily put upon the method of procedure in economic theory.

Economics is essentially *quantitative*. We must therefore always try to get a quantitative conception of everything that is worthy of our attention in economic life. A fundamental requisite for a good economic education, therefore, is a habit of thinking quantitatively, of making up everything in figures. Economic science has indeed suffered seriously from the lack of a quantitative fixing of the ideas under discussion. Authors are far too often satisfied with expressing themselves in vague phrases which commit them to nothing, but which also make nothing clear. Sometimes strong words are used in order to give the impression of something extremely big, and in this way to press a certain opinion upon the reader. This is no truly scientific method of procedure. We must as far as possible strive to build our economic reasoning upon actual figures, even though these may be very approximative. An estimated or even a hypothetical figure is better than none at all, because it helps us to fix our thoughts, binds us in our assumptions with respect to other quantities entering into the problem, and thus prevents us from drawing entirely false conclusions. Estimates in figures are also necessary in order that we may have an idea of the relative importance of the different factors which we have to take into consideration. In economics, quantitative relations are all-important, and we are liable to grave mistakes, and have not much hope of coming to valuable results if we are not able to distinguish, by the aid of quantitative measures, between essential and non-essential factors.

A good example of the usefulness of quantitative thinking in economics is offered by the frequent cases where several causes are responsible for a certain result, and where we have to give an account of these causes. This is of course only possible if we can form a quantitative idea of the effect of each separate cause. Very often this is altogether neglected. Some people are fond of enumerating the greatest possible number of conceivable causes without making any distinction between them, and without paying any attention to the question how they work together. It can then easily happen that we get a superfluity of causes which, taken together, would account for a much greater effect than the actual one which we have to explain!

The general way of proceeding, where different causes which work together to produce a certain result have to be analysed, is this. We have first to find out the most essential causes. Then we have to subtract their joint effect from the total result. Thus only a small margin is left unexplained and a distinct frame is given for further investigations. It may happen that we are not able to get any further, but in most cases further investigations are very much facilitated by this restriction of the field of investigation and by the fact that the unknown, smaller factors can now be regarded in their relation to the essential factors which are known. The familiar example of the so-called Quantitative Theory of Money will make this procedure clear. Obviously the quantity of money required in a community must be primarily dependent upon the quantity of goods to be exchanged and upon the general level of prices, and generally stand in a certain proportion to the product of these factors. It is possible that other factors enter into the problem too. But the analysis of these other factors will be facilitated, and by no means prevented, if, by aid of the quantitative theory, we have first detached the essential factors and their joint effect from the problem. Antagonists of the quantitative theory find pleasure in quoting cases where the actual figures do not seem to harmonize with the theory. They then triumphantly exclaim that it would be very interesting to see the adherents of the quantitative theory explain the case! In such cases it would, in fact, be much more interesting to see the explanation of the opponents. For they would not have the way to a closer analysis of the difficulties cleared up for them by the preliminary separation of the essential factors which the quantitative theory makes possible.

It would not be difficult to quote a long series of examples of the usefulness of quantitative methods in economic theory. Here I must limit myself to point out two further cases of particular importance. First: A theory of interest which is purely qualitative is of very little value. We want to know not only why interest exists, but also why the rate of interest is as high as it is. A theory according to which the rate of interest could just as well be five per mille as five per cent is, after all, no real theory of interest, and in particular can give no sufficient answer to the essential question of the necessity of interest. We can contend that interest is a necessary element in economic life only if we are able to show that the general rate of interest cannot go down permanently beneath a certain figure. In fact, there is such a limit which, on closer examination, proves to have a near connection with the average length of human life. The quantitative method has here demonstrated itself as particularly fertile in putting the very question to be treated in a right form and thus showing the way to a solution.

Again, the theory of foreign exchanges has been very much obscured by the idea that a movement of the rate of exchange between two countries could be explained by an overweighing demand or an overweighing supply. To quantitative thinking it is immediately clear that demand and supply must be equal, i.e., that there must be, for every day, an equal balance of payments between the countries. This simple observation drives us to find a deeper explanation of the relative value of two currencies, and thus we are led to the Purchasing Power Parity Theory.

Decisive importance attaches to the quantitative method in all investigations of dynamic conditions. Such investigations, as I have already explained, must always begin by drawing up the normal curve representing the uniform development. When this is done, the actual movements can be measured as deviations from the normal curve. In such questions we can never be satisfied with qualitative reasoning. E.g., when people have had to explain the influence of the gold supply on general gold prices, they have mostly satisfied themselves with qualitative statements such as: "This period has been characterized by a superabundant supply of gold which has caused a rise of prices." It has, however, never been possible in this way to arrive at a clear analysis of the problem, which is quite natural, because nobody could know what should be meant by a "superabundant supply" or a "very scanty supply," or similar expressions. Only when a curve of normal gold supply for a certain period had been drawn up, representing such a uniform increase of the supply during that period as would leave prices unaltered, was it possible to state for each particular year whether the supply of gold had been normal or abnormal, and, in the latter case, to give a definite measure of the deviation of the supply from the normal. As only this deviation could have any influence on the general level of gold prices, it is immediately clear that in this question only a strict application of quantitative methods could lead to any definite result.

The same holds true with regard to other dynamic problems, first of all, naturally, with regard to the problem of trade cycles. It is impossible to gain an idea of this non-uniform development without first having examined the uniform development. Now, the uniform development is characterized primarily by the uniformity of the growth of capital. This observation already gives the clue to an analysis of the essential feature of the phenomenon of trade cycles, viz., the variations in the volume of construction of capital. Not until we apply quantitative methods and begin to measure these variations can we have the slightest hope of clearing up the different factors which are working together in the movements of trade cycles.

In many practical problems it is important to have some idea of the rate of progress which can be regarded as normal for a modern country. In fact, in qualitative reasonings reference is frequently made to such an idea. E.g., people speak of a very "slow development" or of a period of "unusual prosperity and progress." Statistical investigations have led me to the conclusion that for a Western European country, during the half-century preceding the War, a progress at the rate of three per cent per year, or perhaps a little more, could be regarded as normal. This estimate gives us a distinct quantitative idea of essential relations of the progressive economy, particularly with regard to saving and growth of capital. Of course, objections can be raised against the figures and even against the exact meaning of the very conception of a rate of progress. But, nevertheless, it is far better to have a certain quantitative idea of a matter which is continually the object of so much discussion than to be dependent upon entirely vague phrases.

Finally, let us pay some attention to the way of introducing *definitions* in economic science. In this field, too, an arbitrary way of proceeding and the influence of non-economic points of view have had a pernicious effect. In fact, our science is suffering, with regard to the fixation of conceptions and terminology, from a state of dissolution which may most nearly be described as a state of anarchy. The only way of getting out of this deplorable situation is by the strict observance of the principle that the distinctions and definitions of economic science should be determined by the essential realities of economic life. Scholasticism required that formal definitions should form the entrance to every science. Definitions had then to be made a priori, and thus great scope was unavoidably offered for arbitrariness and irrelevant points of view. Such ideas are entirely incompatible with modern scientific thinking. We should never introduce a name before the thing which has to carry the name is distinctly understood. The first task is therefore an analysis of what is essential in the facts and relations of economic life. Not until this is clear are we able to draw distinctions which correspond to economic essentials, and only then is the time ripe for the introduction of definitions. E.g., the conception of capital should not be introduced a priori. For, as long experience has shown, it is then unavoidable that a complete arbitrariness will prevail in the extent and meaning given to this conception. We must begin with an examination of the economic realities which necessitate the introduction of the conception capital. We are able to do that in quite a clear way only by introducing the two fundamental simplifications of a static and a uniformly progressive economy just referred to.[1]

[1] *The Theory of Social Economy,* pp. 5, 6.

It is, of course, desirable that the language of such a practical science as economic theory should correspond as nearly as possible to that of practical life. However, the vague and changing economic ideas which are current among the public are reflected in a vague and changing language often involving mistakes and contradictions. Therefore, although economic science must try to conserve the nearest possible connection with the language of the business world and the great public, it cannot dispense with the use of its own distinctions and with giving to its terms a more definite meaning.

I have endeavoured here to expound what I think it is most essential to say about the aims and methods of economic theory. These aims and methods afford a very valuable guide to the treatment of the great problems of economic theory. In the following lectures I intend to present some main results of an examination of these problems along the lines here drawn up.

## CHAPTER II

### Economics as a Theory of Price

It has been a very widespread idea that in the exposition of economic theory a separate theory of value ought to go before a theory of price. It seems to have been thought that only in this way was a truly thoroughgoing analysis of economics possible. It was looked upon as a necessity that a student should first make himself familiar with stages of economics where the conception of money was excluded and where the most intricate economic problems had to be handled as if human society did not yet know the use of money. The poor student, who was naturally eager to come forward as soon as possible to a study of the realities of economic life as he knew them from his own experience, had for a long time to renounce such aspirations. Meanwhile, he was trained in reasoning on economic and therefore quantitative questions without clear quantitative conceptions and particularly without the

45

aid of the convenient measure of value which an established monetary unit affords. He had, of course, some difficulty in understanding why he should be deprived of a means of reckoning values which he had become accustomed in his earlier life to regard as indispensable.

I must confess that for my own part this difficulty was quite overwhelming when I first began to study economics. This explains itself, I suppose, partly by my general preference for simplicity and partly by the fact that my earlier training as a mathematician had taught me to be accurate with the elementary arithmetical foundations of scientific thinking. So I was brought from the beginning to ask myself earnestly whether it really was necessary that we should go through such a theory of value, or whether it would not be possible to enter immediately upon the theory of price. My answer was that it ought to be possible to build up a theory of price directly, and that no truth of any importance that could conceivably be explored by the customary theory of value need necessarily be lost by the omission of this theory. In a certain sense I can say that the whole of my scientific work since that time has been devoted to directly building up a theory of price without the use of a separate theory of value, and to working out the consequences of such a way of laying the foundation of economic theory.[1] I shall try to explain here more particularly the motives by which I have been guided in this work.

First of all, economic science had, in my view, to be economical in its own methods, and ought indeed to set an example to all other sciences in economizing in the labour required for attaining essential results. If a difficult theory of value could be dispensed with, and if the student could be introduced more conveniently through the medium of a clear theory of prices to those economic problems which have real importance, it was a primary duty of economic science to achieve this saving of labour.

Further, it was not difficult to see that the theory of value, as mostly exposed in the textbooks and in the lecture-rooms, had its serious drawbacks. The whole theory suffered from an ambiguity in the conception of "value," of which such phrases as "value in use" and "value in exchange" are familiar examples. In

[1] *The Theory of Social Economy,* p. 7.

fact, value always means a price paid under certain circumstances. As the circumstances can be varied *ad libitum,* conceptions of value could be constructed, and indeed actually have been constructed, in great variety, both difficult to survey for the trained economist and extremely bewildering to the young student.

It is really not to the credit of a science that it should not be able to arrive at a general agreement as to its most fundamental conceptions. For this reason it seemed very desirable that it should be possible to build up an economic theory without including value among its elementary conceptions. Great strength was added to this argument when a closer examination revealed how much the theory of value, as it was usually presented, suffered from the lack of a definite unit for measuring the quantities which it had to study. When the value of a thing is described, in the phrase of John Stuart Mill, as "the command which its possession gives over purchasable commodities in general," it must be admitted that such a conception is very little suited as a foundation of an elementary theory with claims on arithmetical clearness and definiteness.

When the so-called "subjective theory of value" appeared and vindicated that value had its foundations in human desires, the need for more definite quantitative conceptions could no longer be neglected. Utility was introduced as the fundamental quantitative conception, and degrees of utility were represented in figures and diagrams. Although the entire body of economic theory had to be built up on such foundations, little attention was generally paid to the necessity of definite units of measurement for the different quantities now introduced into economic science. In modern higher mathematics the arithmetical foundation of the elementary series of whole numbers is looked upon as a most essential thing. Economics cannot do without a corresponding carefulness in defining the units in which it proposes to measure the quantities it is contemplating. Any vagueness in this fundamental point will cause great uncertainty in the interpretation of the results at which the theory has arrived. If, e.g., a theoretical investigation shows that a maximum of utility is attained under certain circumstances, the meaning of this result essentially depends upon the way in which utility has to be measured. The conception of price is in this respect very much superior to the conception of value. For price is measured in money units and can always be represented by definite figures. This fact gives to the whole theory of price a clearness and definiteness which makes it very well suited both as elementary introduction to and as the ultimate foundation of the entire body of economic theory.

Economic science is very much apt to be drawn along false lines, if it does not give from the beginning close attention to its own essential object, and derive its methods and its whole way of proceeding from the nature of that object. If we select arbitrarily a certain conception and make it the purpose of our science to explore that conception, our investigations will in all probability suffer from a great one-sidedness, and we are thus exposed to the risk of being involved in intricate discussions without real importance to the object of our science.

Adam Smith and his followers chose to investigate the nature and causes of the *wealth* of nations, and undoubtedly were driven by this arbitrary choice of the object of their investigations to give undue prominence to wealth and thereby to judgments and representations which we now find one-sided and misleading. In the same way a later school selected arbitrarily the conception of *value* and settled down to analyse this conception. As the word itself is necessarily somewhat vague and is used, in actual language, in a rather varying sense, the scientific analysis was involved in great difficulties, and much time had to be spent in classifications and definitions of different conceptions of value and even in linguistic discussions of the true meaning of the word. It seems in this case more than ever clear that our science has been drawn along a false road. As I explained in my first lecture, the essential object of economic science is economic life, and we shall have the best guidance for our way of proceeding if we direct our efforts from the very beginning towards describing this economic life. It will then be quite natural to study the exchange economy in the money form in which it appears in actual life, and it will seem to be a very artificial and roundabout way first to build up a separate theory of value without the use of a money unit.

One might indeed ask why such a way of

proceeding should ever have been looked upon as a pedagogical necessity. The answer to this question will immediately throw a clearer light upon the whole position of the theory of value. First, people have of course thought that they ought to avoid introducing, at the beginning of an economic treatise, the whole complex theory of money. Therefore they thought it their duty, in their elementary exposition of economics, to do without money. This argument doubtless would carry considerable weight if it were really necessary to work through the whole theory of money before we could allow ourselves to postulate the existence of a unit of money in our exposition of the elements of economics. But, as I shall presently show, the situation is by no means so bad.

Another motive for starting with a separate theory of value has been derived from the idea that a primitive society with exchange of goods but without money has preceded our modern society with its monetary system as the foundation of all exchange. It was thought, more or less consciously, that we ought to follow this social development in our theoretical exposition. The conditions of primitive society were believed to represent the simplest case, which naturally had to be studied first, before the investigation proceeded to the complexities of a society with money. Perhaps it was also thought that by studying such primitive conditions we could penetrate to economic essentials which would escape our analysis if we were to direct our attention immediately to the money economy of modern society.

It was imagined that behind the money form were hidden certain characteristics of value which we could only discover if we studied value independently of money. Mill, for instance, emphasized that all prices could rise simultaneously, but that a general rise of values was logically impossible. On such grounds value ought to be studied for itself, prior to the introduction of the conception of price.

It may be said that these lines of thought in a certain sense coincided with the general rule that we should always in our fundamental investigations introduce a minimum of assumptions with regard to the organizations and the institutions of society. If we observe this rule our results will, as I said in my first lecture, "appear in the full validity which they in fact possess." However, we have no reason to discuss value as an arithmetical conception before we enter upon an investigation of the exchange economy. But as soon as we do that, the object of our investigations is necessarily a society with money or at least with a monetary unit in which values are measured. The postulation of a unit of money, therefore, does not involve any arbitrary limitation of the validity of our results. True, we may find some traces of valuation even in the psychological process which directed primitive man in his isolated household. But they afford no guide to our study of an exchange economy, and we shall understand these primitive processes of valuation much better if we first of all study the corresponding processes in the midst of modern people accustomed to reckoning in money units.

The whole conception of a development of economic life from a barter stage without money to the stage of money economy is doubtless essentially false and has to be ranged among the same concepts as the ideas of "the natural state of things," which were current in the eighteenth century and gave rise to so many descriptions of romantic fascination, but having a very remote connection with historical truth. Just as we have long ago abandoned, in the theory of public life, Rousseau's idea of a "contrat social" and of natural conditions of society preceding it, we ought to abandon in economics the idea of a barter economy preceding the money economy which we know from experience. Money is not a new invention which has been introduced in a society accustomed to a regular exchange of commodities and which has been deliberately accepted by that society. On the contrary, our system of money has been developed *pari passu* with our system of exchange of goods. True, in primitive times we can only find primitive traces of the use of money, but then also we only find primitive traces of the custom of exchange of goods. Certainly there has never existed in the history of human life a society normally dependent upon the exchange of goods without the use of money.[1]

The system of money as we know it is the result of endeavours to satisfy two different

[1] *The Theory of Social Economy,* p. 34.

needs which must have begun to make themselves felt at the earliest stages of the development of the exchange of goods. The first of these needs is the need of a scale for measuring the value of the goods which were to be exchanged or were otherwise to be regarded as equivalent, e.g., in paying taxes and tributes. The idea of an equivalence of certain quantities of different goods goes back to very primitive conditions, although there is then a long way yet to what we would call a valuation in arithmetical terms. Gradually, but probably very slowly, it is found convenient to express such equivalence in the form that different commodities have a value of so and so many units of a certain commodity chosen as a common standard. Different standards have, however, long been used for different·classes of goods, as the idea prevailed that very valuable and durable goods could not be exchanged for less valuable and perishable goods. But gradually such standards have been connected with one another to form a complete scale for the measurement of values. We preserve in modern civilization traces of this development, e.g., in the English custom of reckoning values in three different units, pounds, shillings and pence. Through the stages here described human society has, however, finally arrived at the idea of a unit of value in which the value of all goods could be measured.

This unit of value has always shown a strong tendency to become a more and more abstract unit and to detach itself from the connection with the material thing which originally represented the unit. When, e.g., dried fish are used as units it is of course necessary that the unit should represent a fish of some mean size and quality. Thus the unit became a standard fish, and therefore already to a certain degree an abstraction. This development has often, even in primitive conditions, led to the result that the units in use became entirely abstract units of calculation, and often represented much less value than the material thing which the unit was supposed to denote. In some cases even the original meaning of the unit has been forgotten. The corresponding development of the units of money of modern society is familiar to everybody acquainted with the history of paper currencies.

During this development the need of general means of exchange has been more and more strongly felt. It is conceivable that a primitive system of barter could be carried on by aid of the scale for measuring values which had developed. But the custom of exchange of goods could never become more widespread and more regular before people possessed general means of exchange, which everybody could take in exchange for the goods he had to deliver. The means of exchange which came into use were frequently other things than those which were used as units of value. E.g., people could reckon in oxen as units of value, but use pieces of metal as means of exchange. This is quite natural, as the requirements of a convenient means of exchange are often very different from the requirements of a good standard of value. However, the means of exchange must necessarily have a definite value in the money scale. As the valuation of the means of exchange in the standard unit became fixed by tradition or by the ruling of priests or princes, the actual value represented by the unit came to be determined by the value of the means of exchange, i.e., by their scarcity. Thus the detachment of the unit of money from the thing which it originally represented became complete and the unit was thenceforward a purely abstract unit. The purchasing power of this unit was now determined by the scarcity of the supply of those things which were recognized as means of payment in the existing scale of money. At this stage of the development an actual system of money may be said to have appeared.

Our modern system of money is, therefore, the unification of two devices which have been gradually developed during the very slow progress of the custom of the exchange of goods in order to satisfy the two elementary needs of a unit of value and of a means of exchange.

This analysis of the origin of money makes it clear that the use of a unit of value has been felt to be an elementary need for every society in which the exchange of goods has attained some general importance. If this is so, there is no reason why it should be otherwise for economic science. I think that our science acts wisely in following closely the advice which is here given by the actual development of economic life. Thus, as soon as we decide to study an exchange economy, we have at once to introduce a unit of money in which we can measure all values. The values will then be prices, and we are no longer concerned with a separate conception of value. We can proceed to build up a theory of price without having first to trouble ourselves with a theory of value.

True, there remains the important question: How is the unit of money fixed, what determines its purchasing power, and how can the stability of this unit be guaranteed? These questions cannot be answered at the outset of our study of economics. They must necessarily be deferred to a later exposition of the theory of money. However, our discussion has already shown what is the essential task of this theory: the theory of money has to clear up how the purchasing power of an abstract unit of money is determined.

In our first exposition of the general economic theory we must simply postulate a unit of money as fixed and invariable. If we do that we are able to construct a theory of prices, and the result of this theory is that, in a state of equilibrium, the prices of all goods are determined. However, as they are determined in a unit which is itself left undetermined, it is clear that the prices of goods can only be determined, in the general theory, relatively to one another. This means that the prices of goods are determined except for a multiplicative factor which rests undetermined. This degree of undeterminedness can be removed by fixing absolutely one price. As soon as this is done, all prices are fixed at their absolute level. To explain how this absolute fixation of prices is possible is just the special task of the theory of money, and this is, therefore, a question which must be passed by in an exposition of the general economic theory. When we come later to the theory of money, it will show itself to be a great advantage to have the objects of this theory thus definitely fixed beforehand. The exposition here given of the rôle of the scarcity of the means of payment with regard to fixation of absolute prices already determines the main lines on which the whole theory of money has to proceed.

Once we have chosen to introduce a unit of money in our elementary exposition of the general economic theory, we are bound to construct a theory of money which is suited to this foundation of the general theory. The whole development of the theory of money follows as a logical consequence from the starting-point. In accordance herewith the theory of money which I have gradually built up, and the latest results of which are contained in my analysis of the monetary revolutions of our own time, has been a necessary consequence of the standpoint which I took from the beginning with regard to the theory of value and which is stated already in my first work, *Outlines of an Elementary Theory of Price,* published in the *Tübinger Zeitschrift,* 1899.[1] Nothing in the later development of my theory of money has been arbitrary or a result of influences from other authors. Readers of my book on *The Nature and Necessity of Interest,* which was written in the years 1901 and 1902, and was published the following year,[2] will remember that it already contains the essential foundations of such a theory of money as I have now characterized, and that this theory of money was already conceived as an integral part of a whole system of expounding economic theory.

[1] *Zeitschrift für die gesamte Staatswissenschaft,* Tübingen, 1899.
[2] London, Macmillan, 1903.

As soon as we possess a unit of money, we are able to express in it every valuation of goods which falls within the domain of economic analysis. Thus an economic theory which leaves out the conception of value does not thereby exclude any part or any features of the processes of valuation which could conceivably be explored by a separate theory of value. Indeed, a theory of value which really took its task so earnestly that it gave a true arithmetical form to its discussions, and thus introduced some unit of measure, e.g., of pleasure and pain, or of utility, would *ipso facto* have postulated a unit of money, in the sense of a unit of reckoning value, and would therefore essentially be a theory of price. It is vain, therefore, to oppose the methods of procedure here outlined with the argument that the psychology of valuation would necessarily be neglected by an application of these methods.

Of course, we must give up the idea of any valuation of the unit itself, but this is only of formal importance. For a varying valuation of the unit would, in a system with a fixed unit, take the form of inverse variations in the sums of the unit offered for goods in general. Nor can we take any account of possible alterations in the unit itself. We have postulated a fixed unit and are bound to adhere to this assumption in our general discussion of economic theory. But we do not lose sight of anything by this way of proceeding. The real meaning of alterations in the unit, and therefore also that of the assumption of a fixed unit, only remains to be explained by a theory of money.

Any analysis of a valuation will in our system take the form of a description of the way in which demand depends upon price, i.e., of a representation of demand as a function of price.[1] Demand is, then, just as price, a distinct arithmetical conception, and represents the quantity of the commodity demanded at any given price. Everything that could be said about valuation is shown much more clearly and distinctly by the form of this function. And, what is still more important, the form of this function is all we need to know on the subjective side of the process by which prices are determined, i.e., on the demand side.

A person's demand for a commodity, however, is not only a function of the price of that

[1] *The Theory of Social Economy,* p. 11.

commodity, but also of the prices of all other commodities which come into consideration in his household. In fact, the way in which a person is to use his means can only be fixed when all prices are known. The individual, however, is generally not in the position to form a judgment as to the way in which he would use his means in any given price situation. Practically he is confined to clearing up for himself how much he would buy of a certain commodity at varying prices of that commodity under the assumption that all other prices remained constant. For only under this assumption has the unit a distinct meaning for him. Only in fairly stable conditions, when people by long experience get accustomed to what they can buy for the unit of money, are they able to decide with any certainty how they would alter their demand under the assumption of small variations in one single price. But this also suffices for such a characterization of this demand as is required for the theory of prices. For the best way to study the factors determining prices is to start from the assumption of an equilibrium and to imagine that a small variation takes place in some particular price.

The condition of stability of our equilibrium is that this variation calls forth a reaction in the form of an alteration of the demand in the opposite direction, causing the price to go back again to its original level.

Thus the theory of prices is concerned only with the form of the functions which represent the dependence of demand upon prices of all the different goods. As soon as we take such demand functions into consideration, it is self-evident that we also take account of the increase of demand for a certain article which corresponds to a small decrease of the price of that article. In fact, we do that as soon as we speak of the elasticity of demand. This only means a closer study of the form of the function, a study quite familiar to everybody with the slightest acquaintance with the elementary theory of functions. It seems, therefore, somewhat strange that the application of this method to economic theory should have been praised as a great discovery in our science. The importance of this discovery is particularly emphasized by the school of subjective value. In the endeavours of this school to make utility the foundation of value, it proved necessary to introduce the conception of "marginal utility" in contrast to "total utility," for only this marginal utility would correspond to "value in exchange." But the great importance which has been attributed to this conception of marginal utility was largely artificial, and depended very much on the contrast in which it stood to "total utility," an entirely metaphysical conception without any interest whatever for a simple and straightforward theory of price. When the same school went so far as to declare marginal utility to be the real and ultimate foundation of exchange value, it lost connection with both reality and logic. For, firstly, it is not at all true that marginal utility in every branch of consumption is equal to price. For a well-to-do man it is generally larger in a great number of branches of consumption, which is proved by the fact that he would buy the same amount of a lot of commodities, even if their prices were considerably higher. But secondly, and this is much more important, even when marginal utility and price coincide, marginal utility cannot be represented as the foundation of price, because we never know how much of an article will be consumed, and consequently where the margin lies, before we know the price. Thus the claims of the subjective school to have built up a satisfactory theory of value upon their conception of a marginal utility must be rejected, and the importance of this conception must be reduced to the more modest aspiration of throwing a sidelight upon connections which are essentially known as soon as economic theory has decided to represent demand as a function of price.

On the principles now laid down, economic theory becomes essentially a theory of price. This theory must necessarily embrace the whole process by which prices are determined, and in this process not only prices of the consumers' goods, but also of intermediary goods and of elementary factors of production are included. As people's incomes are determined by the prices of their contributions to production, the whole process which is known in economics as "distribution" is embraced in the theory of prices. This theory, therefore, affords the true frame for a sincere investigation of social questions. When people speak of value from the point of view of social policy, they really mean a price which a thing, e.g., labour, *ought* to have. If such an assertion has any definite meaning, it cannot be that the price in question ought to be other than that which results from the total process of price-fixing, but only that such conditions should be created for this process as would lead to the price in question being fixed at the height regarded as fair. This observation should be of great value for social policy in general, for it shows the way in which true progress can be attained, at the same time as it serves as a serious warning against all sorts of social experiments which are essentially nothing else than an attempt at fixing particular prices in opposition to what the total process of price-fixing requires. Thus the theory of prices becomes also a good guide for social policy.

The substitution of a theory of price for a theory of value has perhaps its most conspicuous advantages when we come to the theory of interest on capital.[1] If we keep strictly to the standpoint of the theory of value, we shall be obliged to present a complete explanation of

[1] Cf. *Nature and Necessity of Interest,* and *The Theory of Social Economy,* chap. vi.

the phenomenon of interest on the grounds of the formula of Boehm-Bawerk, that there is a general undervaluation of future goods in comparison with present ones, and that interest is an agio paid in the exchange between present and future goods. It cannot perhaps be said that it is logically impossible to mould the theory of interest in this form. For it is undoubtedly true that in a certain sense a contract involving paying of interest represents an exchange between present and future goods. However, it must be very seriously doubted whether this form of explanation is advantageous, and whether from any point of view it is preferable to the explanation which naturally presents itself within the frame of a general theory of prices. It is clearly very desirable that a theory of interest should reflect as truly as possible the transactions which in real life lead up to the payment of interest. From this point of view the formula of Boehm-Bawerk must be regarded as extremely artificial.

When we try to work out a theory of interest on the grounds of this formula, we inevitably become involved in difficulties which, though perhaps not quite insuperable, are nevertheless unnecessary. I wish particularly to point out here that there is in reality no "general undervaluation" of future goods. It is quite certain that wealthy people would not immediately consume all their wealth if no interest were obtainable. They would even then save some part of their wealth for future consumption. Indeed, they would do that even if they had to pay a "negative interest" for a possibility of preserving their wealth for years to come. In such cases an overvaluation of future goods takes place. On the other hand, nobody would exchange *all* his present goods for future ones even if he were compensated by the highest rate of interest. Thus the undervaluation of future goods cannot, even in the case of an individual, be expressed by a single figure. It is therefore also impossible to speak of an "average undervaluation" in the society. In fact, our undervaluation of future goods can be clearly described only in the form of a dependence of our economic dispositions upon the rate of interest. The market for the exchange between present and future goods is brought to equilibrium only by a certain rate of interest, and it is just this market which should be the primary object of a theory of interest. It must be confessed that such a study is made extremely difficult by putting the problem in the form of an exchange between present and future goods.

The whole problem becomes much more natural and intelligible when we choose to regard interest as a price and when the theory of interest is therefore included as an integral part of the general theory of prices.

For this purpose it is first of all necessary to clear up the question of what is the elementary factor of production for which interest is paid. Capital, in the sense of produced material goods, is no elementary factor of production, as these goods are themselves produced. It may be said that interest is the price paid for the use of this capital. But then the question arises, how the price of the capital itself is determined, and clearly, the problem of interest coincides exactly with the question of how the proportion between the price of the use and the price of the capital itself is determined. In order to answer this question we must follow the way indicated by actual economic practice. We know that people pay interest as a compensation for the right of using a certain sum of money for a certain time, and the scientific analysis has simply to build directly on this fact. The use of £100 for a year is an elementary factor of production, and the price paid for the co-operation of this factor is interest. This price is, e.g., £4 2s. 6d., and is thus, according to English customs, really expressed in terms of money.

The theory of interest has then first to explain why the use of an abstract capital for a certain time is a necessary factor of production. This explanation is simple enough if we only direct our attention to the analysis of actual economic life. Production in a technical sense takes time, and the wearing out of durable goods takes generally much more time. Therefore time must elapse between the sacrifice of factors of production and the compensation paid for this sacrifice. In the meantime it is necessary to have a corresponding amount of money at disposal. The continual social economy must constantly possess a certain amount of abstract capital corresponding to the total value of all the material goods within the process of production. The continual disposition over this abstract capital is therefore a necessary factor of production. It is particularly useful to make this observation because it then at once becomes clear that even for a socialist community the possession of this factor of production is a necessity.

In the general process of price-fixing this factor obtains a price on the same grounds as other elementary factors of production. I shall have to explain these grounds in my next lecture, and therefore shall confine myself here to some remarks of particular importance for a true understanding of the problem of interest as a price problem.

When the rate of interest, as well as all other prices, is fixed, everybody possesses the data which he requires for the planning of his economy. He knows how much of his income he wishes to consume at present, and how much he can set aside for future needs or simply for increasing his capital. Thus the total amount of saving in the society is determined, and therefore the additional amount of disposition over capital that is offered on the market in any period is known.

It remains, however, to take account of the consumption of capital which is carried on by people who, for one reason or another, consume more than their actual income. This consumption of capital represents what we could call a "negative saving." If we subtract this negative saving from the positive saving, we have the net saving of the society. Only this net saving will supply disposition over capital to the process of production. These definitions are convenient and suitable for the clearest and most natural exposition of the supply side of our problem. Some authors proceed in a different way and add the consumption of capital here referred to to the demand for disposition over capital which has its origin in the process of production. We cannot perhaps say that this way of proceeding is wrong. But it does certainly not reflect the real occurrences of which we have here to take account in the most natural way, and is, therefore, very little suited for giving a clear survey of the elements of the problem before us. Indeed, saving and over-consumption are, after all, only different sides of one and the same planning of a person's economy. In most cases these different sides are also logically connected with one another, as over-consumption must be paid by later savings, or has already been paid by earlier savings. It must, therefore, be recognized as very natural to calculate the net saving of the society, and regard this as the real supply of capital put at the disposal of production.

The net saving of the society is obviously dependent upon the rate of interest, and we may assume that it is determined as soon as the rate of interest is given. What in Boehm-Bawerk's terminology must be taken in a rather vague sense as a more or less extended undervaluation of future goods in comparison with present ones is now expressed in a distinct arithmetical way, viz., in the amount of net savings of the society that are put at the disposal of production at each rate of interest. The superiority of the theory of price over the theory of value is hereby proved with convincing clearness.

At a very low rate of interest the consumption of capital must assume extraordinary proportions, simply because a man who has twenty-five years more to live can have 4 per cent of his capital at his disposal every year if he chooses to consume the whole capital during the said period. This simple observation points to the true reason why the rate of interest is somewhere about 4 per cent, and cannot equally well be, say, somewhere about 4 pro mille. A close investigation into this subject, founded on the statistics of probable expectation of life and on our knowledge of the distribution of wealth between the different classes of age, reveals the very interesting connection between the rate of interest and the length of human life.

The rate of saving in any society is intimately connected with its rate of progress. In our present economic organization progress is determined by the net savings of the individual households. In a socialistic community it would be determined by the organized society itself. But even then there would exist narrow limits to the desire to sacrifice present satisfaction for progress. Thus the net supply of saving has always its limits.

On the demand side we have, according to what has now been said, only to take account of the needs of production for disposition over capital. This demand, of course, like all other demands for factors of production, has its origin in the consumer's demand for ready-made products and services. Now, the price paid for disposition over capital has a very important influence on the relative prices of consumer's goods. For the production of these goods requires very different amounts of disposition over capital, and an increase in the rate of interest must, therefore, increase the price of some goods, e.g., house-rents and rail-way-fares, in a particularly high degree. Thus the consumer's demand is materially affected by alterations in the rate of interest, and always reacts against such alterations, so that an increase in the rate of interest causes a reduction of the consumer's indirect demand for disposition over capital and *vice versa*. This fact is essential for the explanation of the stability of the capital market. It is extremely difficult to see how it should be possible to give a clear account of these connections within the frame of the formula of an exchange between present and future goods.

The rate of interest cannot be lower than it actually is, because the consumer's indirect demand for disposition over capital would then become greater than the supply. This is the kernel of the theory of interest. The consumers compete with one another for disposition over capital, and thus drive up the price of this disposition to a certain height. This way of presenting the problem seems to be well suited for clarifying the practical business man's ideas of interest and for bringing them into touch with scientific analysis. At the same time it shows immediately that the necessity of interest is not confined to the present organization of society, but has its root in the impossibility of satisfying every demand for disposition over capital. Thus the price theory of interest arrives at much more definite results in the matter of the necessity of interest than were attainable by aid of the earlier value theory.

# CHAPTER III

## The Principle of Scarcity and the Conception of Cost

Economy means procuring for human needs under the condition that there is a certain scarcity in the means for satisfying these needs. Thus in every economy needs have to be restricted, demands have to be cut short, so far that they can be satisfied by aid of the available means. This is the Principle of Scarcity. In a self-supporting isolated family the task is accomplished simply by the will of the leader who regulates the whole consumption of the household. It is conceivable that the same could be done in a society organized on communistic principles. In the exchange economy there is no central authority regulating demand. The characteristic of the exchange economy is the freedom of choice of consumption enjoyed by every individual within the limits of his total purchasing power. This freedom of consumption is a thing on which

people place a very high value, although they
are generally not conscious of it because they
regard such freedom as self-evident. But as
even in the exchange economy it is impossible
to satisfy all demands, it is necessary that the
exchange economy should possess a means for
suitably restricting the demands. This means
is price. When a price is put on a certain
article, only such demand as is prepared to
pay the price will be satisfied, and all other
demands are cut off. Thus demand is restricted to correspond to the supply. This is
the Principle of Scarcity in the form it takes
in the exchange economy. We see that prices
have a distinct social function to fulfil. Their
purpose is to restrict demand in every line so
much that it can be satisfied by the supply available. Prices must be so high that this end can
be attained.

This is the core of the theory of prices which
I have developed in my different writings, and
which in fact forms the basis of my whole economic work. There is no arbitrariness in the
construction of this theory. It has its basis
indeed in the fundamental fact of every economy, namely, the scarcity of the means for sat-

isfying human needs, and it is a true expression of the solution which exchange economy has given to the fundamental problem of every economy, namely, the restriction of the needs to correspond with this scarcity.

The objection has been made against my theory that it represents the whole system of prices as having been constructed for a certain purpose, and I have been accused of having in this way introduced into economics an element of teleology which ought to be kept out of science. This objection does not carry much weight. We are all accustomed to speak in corresponding terms about the most common occurrences in natural science. E.g., we say that the heart has the function of driving the blood through the body, and that the purpose of respiration is to supply oxygen to the blood. We do not mean by such expressions to take any standpoint on the question of the teleology of nature. We simply use a convenient way of stating the function of different organs. We can do the same thing in economics, and we can do it with great advantage. It would indeed be very wholesome for people in general to make themselves acquainted with the thought that prices have the distinct purpose of cutting off demand and that they fulfil an important social function by so doing. For people often complain of the deplorable fact that demand has been cut off by a rise of price, and then they are only too ready to urge that the Government should step in and forbid the price to rise. But if the authorities do that, they disturb the whole mechanism by which prices are fixed in the exchange economy and create conditions under which it is impossible to satisfy demand by aid of the existing supply. The consequence is simply that the necessary restriction of demand must be attained by irregular and generally very irrational methods.

The means of restricting demand by putting a sufficiently high price on the article demanded cannot be applied in all cases. True, most needs are individual, and can be restricted by making the payment of a certain price the condition for the satisfaction of the need. But this is not always so. Certain needs are in their nature collective, i.e., they are needs of a collective body, needs which can only be satisfied for the body as a whole. Once such a need is satisfied, no individual belonging to the body can be excluded from enjoying the satisfaction. It is therefore impossible to make the payment of a certain price the condition for supplying the individual with the good in question. A typical case is the need for defence against contagious diseases. Once protective measures have been taken for a country, all the inhabitants of that country have the advantage of them. They cannot be excluded from enjoying this advantage, and thus it is impossible to ask the individual to pay for his share of the benefit. The difficulty is overcome by forming a compulsory organization of all inhabitants and forcing them to pay contributions to this organization in order that the organization may be able to pay for the necessary protection. The greatest of all such compulsory organizations is the State, but we have a whole series of local bodies of a similar character. Their essential function is to provide for collective needs, in the distinct sense here given to this term. They collect taxes and rates, and by this means pay all the expenses for satisfying the collective needs of their members. Of course, the collective demands themselves are restricted by the prices which the collective bodies have to pay for the goods they wish to have. In this way the collective bodies are put on the same footing as the individual demanders of goods within the total exchange economy. State and municipal finance can with great advantage be treated from the point of view of the theory of collective goods which I have developed on the lines now indicated, and which immediately clears up both the essential economic character of our public organizations and the true place of public finance within the general exchange economy of the society.

After having in this way placed the public bodies in their right place as consumers, we can give general validity to our thesis that the function of prices is to restrict demand in every line to conform with supply. This formula then becomes the starting-point for the general explanation of the process by which prices are fixed in an exchange economy.

The fixing of prices is not the only possible way of restricting demand. Demand can be regulated by laws forbidding people to consume more than certain quantities. In fact, this was done on a large scale during the war by the system of rationing. But this way of restricting is, as everybody now knows from sad experience, extremely disagreeable and extremely expensive. In future, society will only have recourse to such methods for the regulation of individual demand when it is forced to adopt them owing to extraordinary circumstances. This does not, of course, exclude the possibility that a system of rationing may be used regularly, as it actually is in Sweden, for the restriction of a pernicious consumption, such as that of alcoholic liquors. The rule for a developed exchange economy, however, must be that demand be regulated only by the prices it has to pay.

Suppose the supply of consumer's goods to be given in fixed quantities, and, in addition, suppose the money incomes of the consumers to be fixed. We then have the simplest case for studying how prices are determined in accordance with the Principle of Scarcity. As soon as a price is put upon each of the consumer's goods, every consumer knows how he will dispose of his income, i.e., how much he wishes to buy of each of the goods. Thus the total demand within the society for each of the consumer's goods is determined. This demand must—in a state of equilibrium—be equal to the supply. We have as many such conditions or equations as there are different consumers' goods, and thus these conditions suffice for determining all the prices at once.

There is no simpler way of expounding the process by which prices are fixed. For as the individual's demand for a particular good is generally dependent, not only on the price of this good but also—at least to some extent— on the prices of all other goods, it is impossible to solve the price problem merely by stating that the price of each good must reduce the demand for it to equality with the supply.

Let us now leave the assumption that the supply of consumers' goods is fixed, and let us take account of the fact that these goods can be produced. Then there is no absolute scarcity of these goods. Instead, we are thrown back upon the scarcity of elementary means of production which cannot themselves be produced. We then make the assumption that the supply of these elementary factors of production is given in fixed quantities. Thus they exist in absolute scarcity, and the Principle of Scarcity can be applied to them. In fact, the demand for consumer's goods is now an indirect demand for elementary factors of production, and therefore the Principle of Scarcity leads to a solution of the problem in a similar way.

Supposing that there is a certain price for each factor of production, and supposing that we know how much of each of these factors is required in order to produce a unit of each of the consumers' goods, it follows that the prices of the consumers' goods will also be known. Then the consumers are in a position to fix their demand, and we therefore know how much of each of the consumer's goods will be demanded. But then the quantities of the elementary factors of production required to produce these quantities of consumers' goods are also known. Now, this demand for the elementary factors of production must, for each factor, be equal to the fixed supply of it, and thus we have as many conditions or equations as there are unknown quantities in the problem, viz., the prices of the elementary factors of production. These conditions suffice to fix these prices. Our whole system of equations is now determined, and thereby the whole price problem is solved. For now we know also the price of each of the con-

sumer's goods and therefore the demand for
them. But then again we see how the different
factors of production are disposed of. They
are drawn, in proportions which are now
known, to the production of the different consumers' goods, and so much of each of these
goods will be produced as is required for satisfying the demand.

This analysis, which I have more fully
worked out in my *Theory of Social Economy,*
where also I have given to it the necessary
mathematical form,[1] already reveals the essential character of the process by which prices are
fixed. But, of course, it is incomplete and must
be further developed. In particular, we have to
give up the assumption that the money incomes
of the consumers are fixed. In reality the incomes of the individuals in an exchange economy are determined by the prices of those
elementary factors of production which they
contribute to the process of production. This
circumstance must, of course, make the system
of equations of the price problem a little more
complicated, but it does not alter the essential
character of our solution. Our system of equa-

[1] Chaps. iii and iv.

tions will henceforward determine not only the prices of consumers' goods, and of the elementary factors of production, but also the incomes of all the members of the society, and therewith the entire social distribution of income.

In the further development of our analysis we shall also have to take account of the fact that the present demand for consumers' goods is not in general a present demand for elementary factors of production. In most cases a certain time elapses between the moment when a factor of production is introduced into the productive process and the moment when the final product, in which this factor has collaborated, reaches the consumer. The complications which arise out of this circumstance can only be cleared up if we make the continual process of production the object of our investigations. Here the importance, indeed, the necessity, of this conception shows itself in a particularly convincing way. In the continuing economy we have to do with a continuing demand for consumers' goods, requiring a continuing supply of elementary factors of production, and we must know the connection between this demand and this supply. In the static stage where there is no progress, the total demand for earlier factors of production which originates in the demand for consumers' goods during a present unit of time is equal to that total demand for this period's factors of production which is derived from the whole future demand for consumers' goods. We may therefore speak of the demand for consumers' goods simply as if it were an immediate demand for elementary factors of production. This is not so in the progressive society. There the latter demand, as coming from later periods, is necessarily greater than the former one, which represents present consumption. This is a fact of which we have to take account also in practical life. We have always to reckon with greater claims on our present productive power than those which would correspond to our present satisfaction of wants. The will to meet such claims is the essential characteristic of a progressive society. This will must express itself, in one way or another, in a certain degree of saving, which indeed determines the rate of progress. We may, for the sake of simplicity, assume this rate to be constant, and we have then to deal with a uniformly progressive economy. In order to be able to provide for a uniformly growing consumption we must, in this economy, have a uniformly growing supply of elementary factors of production. In this case the supply required in the present unit of time does not only depend on consumers' demand in this period, but also on the rate of progress. But as soon as this rate is fixed, the present requirements of the factors of production are determined by the present demand for consumers' goods. We can then proceed as before with our solution of the problem of price-fixing.

Consumers cannot, of course, be expected to pay for more of the present supply of factors of production than would correspond to present consumption. The rest of the factors of production is paid for by the savers. Thus it is seen clearly how savings determine the rate of progress. The total income of the society in any unit of time is equal to the total price of the factors of production supplied in that period. But, as this supply in the progressive economy outgrows the supply which would correspond to the consumption within the same period, the income of the society is greater than the total price of its consumption. The rate of the income represents the savings of the period, and goes to buy the additional real capital produced in the same period.

We have assumed in our exposition of the price theory that the price of any product is known as soon as the prices of the required factors of production are known. In reality there is a series of exceptions from this rule which we have to take account of in the complete theory. Of these I shall here mention only two of the most essential, viz., the cases where there are different costs in different undertakings required for supplying the demand, and the cases where variation can take place in the relative quantities of the factors used in the production of a certain commodity. In such cases the Principle of Scarcity is not sufficient to make the price problem determinable. It is, therefore, necessary to introduce certain supplementary principles. These principles are all ultimately derived from the general principle that a maximum of economy should be attained, and, therefore, have the same validity as this principle. They are, in the cases here referred to, the Differential Principle and the Principle of Substitution. The Differential Principle tells us that the price of the product must correspond to the highest cost of any undertaking required for satisfying the demand. The undertakings working with lower costs have then a differential advantage which commands its own price, usually called a differential rent, and these rents will level out the costs of the different undertakings. The Principle of Substitution tells us that among all conceivable relations between the various quantities of the factors used in production, that one should be chosen which minimizes the cost of production. Both these principles are well known to every student of economics, and I wish here only to emphasize their character of supplementary principles, modifying the fundamental Principle of Scarcity, but not supplanting it. The scarcity of fertile land is modified when less fertile land can be taken into use for satisfying the demand for food. But the reason why a fertile piece of land has a price is by no means the existence of less fertile land. When economic textbooks express themselves as if this were the case, one can hardly help being reminded of the saying that pins have saved innumerable lives by not being swallowed! Likewise, the scarcity of one kind of fodder is modified by the possibility of substituting it by other fodders for feeding cattle. But as long as all fodders are scarce, their scarcity is the fundamental fact of the economy of cattle-feeding. The ultimate and essential reason, on the supply side, why a price is paid for a fodder is that it is scarce, not that it may be supplanted by another fodder.

By the introduction of these and other supplementary principles, required in particular cases to fix the cost of production, the whole price problem becomes determined. We find that prices are governed by the given factors of the problem, and fundamentally by the scarcity of the means for satisfying wants in comparison with the intensity of these wants.

One might now ask: What is the use of giving a complicated system of equations as the solution of the price problem? We cannot solve these equations and by aid of them actually calculate the prices. What do we then win by our treatment of the problem? In my opinion we win very important advantages.

The first essential advantage of our system of

equations is that it displays the true nature of the connection between causes and effects in the price problem. Our solution of the problem immediately shows us that all prices are determined at once, and that there is no order of precedence between different groups of prices with regard to their position as cause and effect. The true determining elements of the price problem are the given quantities in our system of equations. There are three main groups of such quantities: First, the quantities characterizing the dependence of demand upon prices of consumer's goods; second, the technical coefficients which determine the cost of production in a technical sense; and, third, the supply of the elementary factors of production which we have taken to be given in definite quantities. The first group may be denoted as the subjective, the second and third together as the objective elements of the price problem. These elements form the ultimate basis for the determining of prices. They have all the same importance for the problem, and we cannot speak of any order of precedence between them. Thus, an objective or a subjective theory of value which would attribute a preponderance to the objective elements on the supply side, or to the subjective elements on the demand side, is an impossibility, excluded in advance by our treatment of the problem.

Once the determining elements of the price problem have been given, all the unknown quantities of the problem are determined simultaneously. This truth does not only apply to the prices, but also to the quantities of the different factors of production used in different lines of production, and therefore also to their "marginal productivity," the quantities of each of the consumers' goods produced, the extent to which every demand is satisfied, and therefore also to the "marginal utilities" of all products, and so on. It is hereby particularly made clear that any theory which represents "marginal productivity" or "marginal utility" as determining prices is mistaken. We may introduce these conceptions if we find them convenient, but we should always remember that they have their place within the frame of our system of equations, and that they can never render this system superfluous. Modern economists have pointed out that all the unknowns of the price problem mutually govern one another. This observation has been useful in order to clear up the mistake of schools which have attributed the determining influence in the price problem to one or another set of unknowns in the problem. But we should be careful lest the new conception of a mutual interdependence lead to new misunderstandings. The unknowns of the problem cannot in a true sense be said to govern one another. None of them has a sufficient independence for exercising such a governing influence. In reality, they are all governed and simultaneously determined by those elements of the problem which we have characterized as elementary and which we have taken as given.

The second great advantage of our system of equations is closely connected with the first. It is that it gives to the Principle of Scarcity its true place in the theory of prices. In the first stage of our investigation the scarcity in the supply of the consumers' goods is taken as fixed and constitutes a set of given factors in the problem. In the second stage the same place is taken by the scarcity of the elementary factors of production, which are now assumed to be supplied in definite quantities. We may

go a step further and also take into consideration the influence which prices may exercise on
the supply of the elementary factors of production. Then the scarcity of these factors is
no longer absolute, but it does not therefore
entirely disappear. It is only substituted by
the slowness with which the supply is increased
in response to a rise in prices. Thus the scarcity may alter its form, but it always retains its
place as a given factor in the problem.

By this treatment in successive stages of the
great process of price-settlement it is possible
at every stage to arrive at definite results. We
avoid difficulties which are necessarily connected with any attempt to treat the whole price
problem all at once. Of course, as we go
through the different stages of our investigation, the circle of our unknowns is enlarged,
and comes to comprise factors which have been
regarded as given at the foregoing stage. But
at every stage the unknowns are determined by
the factors which at that stage are taken as
given, and thus a definite distinction is maintained between the given factors and the unknowns which are to be determined by them.
This definiteness of conceptions is a great step

forward in comparison with the rather loose idea of a general "mutual dependence."

A third great advantage which we derive from our system of equations is that we see that an equilibrium of prices exists, and how this equilibrium is determined. We clearly see what forces counteract any disturbances of this equilibrium. We are in the position to state the consequences, say, of a fall of a price. Supposing the price of an elementary factor of production to have been reduced by a small fraction, the result will be a corresponding reduction in the prices of all products in which this factor of production enters. Thus the consumers' demand of these products is increased. It will be necessary, therefore, to produce more of them. This means, however, an increased demand for the elementary factor of production in question. But as the whole supply of it was already before required for the production, it is impossible to satisfy this new demand. The demand has to be restricted by a sufficiently high price. The price of the factor must therefore rise again, and thereby the equilibrium from which we started is restored. If, e.g., the rate of interest should be lowered a fraction beneath what it actually is in a state of equilibrium, the result would be an increased demand for such commodities as require much disposition over capital for their being supplied to the consumers. House rents, railway fares, and rates for electric energy would become cheaper, and the demand for these commodities would increase, with the result that the total demand for disposition over capital would outgrow the supply. Then the rate of interest would have to be raised again in order that it should be able to cut off such demand as could not be satisfied. This very essence of a rational theory of interest is usually put in the background, not to say entirely neglected, because the Principle of Scarcity is not given its due place in the explanation.

Thus the fundamental reason why an elementary factor of production must have a price is that otherwise the consumers' indirect demand for it would outgrow the supply. By this statement the futility of a "labour theory of value"—according to which the value of a product would be determined solely by the labour it has cost to produce—is proved in the simplest and most conclusive way. The price

has, as we see here, and as I have explained
before, the essential function of restricting the
demand so that it can be satisfied by the supply,
which is supposed to be given in a definite
scarcity. This is the Principle of Scarcity. It
may be said, perhaps, that this principle is
nothing else than the old familiar theory of
demand and supply. In a certain sense this
is true. Still, I think it is useful to emphasize,
in the way I have done, the essential importance for every economy of the scarcity of the
means which it has at its disposal for providing
for its wants. The existence of such a scarcity
is the fundamental fact which makes economizing necessary, and we ought, therefore, to give
this scarcity its due central position in our
economic theory. From the very beginning of
my studies of economics I had a feeling that in
this respect something was wanting. True, attention has been paid to scarcity in discussions
of market conditions. Here writers have been
agreed that price is determined by demand and
supply, and in this we can trace a certain recog-
nition of the Principle of Scarcity. But it is
characteristic that this view of the matter, and
therewith the whole Principle of Scarcity, is

forced into the background, and indeed in most cases entirely disappears, as soon as the analysis of the price-problem has to be carried further and to include also the prices of the ultimate factors of production.

The first comprehensive effort at building up a general theory of prices was made by Ricardo. When he comes to answer the question what determines prices ultimately and in the long run, he adopts a cost-of-production theory. But a theory which refers prices of commodities to the costs of production has at the end to face the question, how then the prices of the elementary factors of production are fixed in relation to one another. For these factors the cost-of-production explanation fails, and a consistent cost-of-production theory of prices is therefore logically impossible, except when there is only one factor of production. Now Ricardo's whole theory must, as I have explained in a paper in the *Tübinger Zeitschrift* of 1901,[1] be looked upon as a great effort to reduce to one the number of the factors of production of which the theory of price has

[1] *Die Produktionskostentheorie Ricardo's. Zeitschrift für die gesamte Staatswissenschaft.* Tübingen, 1901.

to take account, and thereby to make his cost-of-production theory possible. This single factor of production in the Ricardian system is labour. Land as a factor of production is eliminated from the theory of price by the well-known Ricardian artifice of letting the whole process of price-fixing be carried out on the margin of cultivation where no rent of land is paid, and capital is eliminated by the somewhat daring simplification that the use of capital required in every branch of production could be assumed to be proportional to the amount of labour required. Thus Ricardo arrives at the result that the prices of all goods are proportional to their labour cost of production.

The reasoning is logical, but a little too abstract, and it has done immense harm by being misinterpreted. Particularly the labour theory of value, which has become the foundation-stone of modern socialism, is, as I have shown, a direct result of misinterpretations of the Ricardian doctrine. The simplifications on which Ricardo's theory is built are so violent that the theory must be unable to offer a fair representation of what really happens in the actual process of price-fixing. The worst of it is that Ricardo's theory cannot be improved or further developed by modifying his fundamental simplifications. For as soon as we do that we must give up the essential assumption on which the whole theory is built, viz., that there is only one factor of production to take account of in the theory of prices, and as soon as we are faced with the existence of different factors of production, the Ricardian cost-of-production theory becomes, as I have said, logically impossible.

It remains to explain how, in Ricardo's system, the price of labour and the price of disposition over capital can be determined in relation to one another. The division of the result of one hour's labour between wages and profits is in Ricardo's system determined by the fact that both labour and accumulation of capital are to some extent withdrawn, if not properly remunerated. Here the unwillingness of human agents of production to supply their services except at a certain price is introduced as an independent factor in the price-problem. In this we have the starting-point for the efforts of later theories to determine the prices of elementary factors of production, and thus to be able to build up a general theory of prices without being obliged to reduce the number of factors of production to one.

In opposition to former cost-of-production theories the later school of subjective value has asserted that all value had its root in the subjective demand of the members of the society, and that this subjective demand had to be made the foundation of the theory of prices. The fundamental shortcoming of this school is exposed by the fact that they thought it a contradiction to speak of several different sets of factors working together in the determination of a price. The kind of thinking to which such a connection is entirely foreign, is, of course, unable to form a clear idea of the machinery by which the exchange economy fixes prices, even if it may prove sharp enough in discussing particular sides of the problem.

Among modern writers Marshall has undoubtedly taken the most comprehensive view of the price-problem. In his theory there is no one-sidedness. He gives just as much prominence to the factors working on the supply side as to those working on the demand side. He may be said to have built further on the foundation laid by Ricardo, but he made use of all the results of later economic thinking. How, then, has he overcome the fundamental difficulty of the Ricardian system, viz., the fact that we must reckon with several different factors of production, and that, therefore, the reduction of all costs to one common measure is impossible? As soon as we have to deal with several elementary factors of production we have to make clear what it is that determines their prices. Marshall's answer to this question is that for some factors of production a certain price must be paid in order to call forth an adequate supply. The factors in question are all human, and the prices must be paid in order to induce the human will to do something. The manner in which human will responds to the price offered is then a new elementary factor in the price-problem. It is the introduction of these elementary factors which makes it possible for Marshall to develop the Ricardian cost-of-production theory into a comprehensive theory of prices more truly reflecting the realities of economic life.

The two great factors of production which Marshall is able to treat in this way are labour and saving. Obviously the method applies also to different kinds of labour, and thus it is possible to overcome the difficulty experienced by the earlier economists in reducing different kinds of labour to a common measure. For every kind of labour a price must be paid, sufficient to compensate the "efforts and sacrifices" required for doing the work and for acquiring the necessary skill for the purpose. Likewise a price must be paid for saving or "waiting" in order to compensate for the "efforts and sacrifices" involved in the waiting. These efforts and sacrifices constitute in Marshall's system the real costs, and the total price that has to be paid for them is the cost of production in terms of money. Marshall's solution of the price-problem is now built upon these costs of production as the determining factors on the supply side.

On closer consideration of this solution we are struck by the fact that the non-human factors of production are entirely left out. In this Marshall has followed Ricardo. The price-problem is studied on the margin of cultivation where no rent of land is paid, and therefore no such rent is enclosed in the costs of production or in the prices of products. A widening of this principle allows Marshall to eliminate all differential incomes or "quasirents" from the price-fixing process. There then remain to be taken into account within this process only those human factors of production whose supply is dependent upon their price. Thus the whole theory seems to be complete.

This great achievement of a wonderfully constructive genius, however, is, with all its merits, undoubtedly not a little artificial. First, the assumption that the supply of labour and saving is increased in response to an increase of price has in Marshall's system quite a fundamental importance which has no correspondence in reality. Even if it were true that a supply of the said factors of production to some extent varies with the price paid for them, this circumstance can never be regarded as an essential condition for the possibility of a solution of the general price-problem. Our most natural instinct tells us that it ought to be possible to build up a theory of price even if the quantities of labour and saving supplied were fixed and independent of variations in the prices of these factors. Indeed, in a broad general exposition of the price-problem, this is the most natural simplifying assumption to start from. In a society such as ours, where the eight-hour day is often legally enforced, and where the intensity of work is largely regulated by trade unions, it is certainly somewhat daring to make the dependence of the supply of labour on the price paid for it one of the foundation stones of the general theory of prices. We are simply obliged to show how the process of price-fixing works in a society where the supply of labour is rigidly fixed. Likewise, the amount of saving supplied in our actual society is certainly not so much dependent on the price paid for it that any prominence whatever should be attributed to this dependence when we have to lay the very foundations of our economic theory. The theory must be able to answer its essential questions even if saving were in reality independent of small variations in the rate of interest. If we put these claims upon our theory, the principle of scarcity will appear as its fundamental principle. The fact that prices are paid for such services as are included under the heads of "labour" and "saving" then proves to be a result simply of the scarcity of the supply of these services, the prices having the function of cutting down the demand for them to equality with the supply. This explanation has the essential merit of absolute objectiveness. It entirely excludes every shade of that moral justification for a price which has played such an unfortunate rôle in the development of economic science and given such an unnecessarily controversial character to the question of social distribution. It makes it clear that a price is paid for a factor of production not primarily because the owner of the factor asks for that price or makes the payment of it a condition of his service, but essentially because of the scarcity of the factor in relation to the demand for it. This Principle of Scarcity is thrust into the background in Marshall's theory. But thereby our attention is withdrawn from the most essential side of the whole price-problem.

Secondly, the result of this way of proceeding is a dualism in the fundamental explanation of the settlement of prices: some factors of production are acknowledged to have their own supply prices, and are, therefore, fully recognized as determining elements in the process of

price-fixing, but the remaining factors of production are, by a clever use of the differential
principle, simply shut out from the whole
process. I have always felt that this is extremely artificial, and that it must be possible
to give all the different factors of production
a symmetrical position in the great process by
which prices are settled.

This is done by our system of equations.
Land of a certain quality gets its price on
account of its scarcity just as well as any
human factor of production. All the elementary factors of production are placed on the
same footing in the general process of price-
fixing, and their prices are all determined
simultaneously. This view of the problem
leads, of course, to a new conception of cost.
Expressed in money terms, cost can now only
be the sum of all the prices which have to be
paid for the different factors of production required. This conception is purely objective.
It only takes account of the fact that prices
have to be paid, and it entirely leaves out the
question whether these prices represent a compensation for "efforts and sacrifices" or not.
Essentially, prices are paid for elementary

factors of production because they are supplied in a certain scarcity. Costs are therefore primarily simply an expression for scarcity. But the new conception of cost is sufficiently wide and objective to be valid independently of the different influences which may have made themselves felt in fixing prices. Cost should in any case only mean the sum of prices that actually has to be paid. It follows that a price paid for the use of land in a certain production enters into the cost of the food produced. If a similar production is carried on on a second piece of land where other costs are higher, the price of the use of this land must be so much lower that the whole cost of production is equal to what it was in the former case and equal to the price of the product. Here the Differential Principle comes in, but it enters only as a supplementary principle, subordinate to the general Principle of Scarcity, and helping to make the price-problem determined. With the solution of this problem all costs become known, among them also the cost of using such and such a piece of land. These remarks are perhaps sufficient to clear up the main lines of the theory of cost at which we arrive by proceeding in this way. For a more complete explanation I must refer to my main work on the subject.

In my opinion it must be regarded as an essential advantage that the conception of cost thus defined corresponds closely to the general business man's idea of cost. A producer has to pay for the co-operation of different factors of production. For him every sum of money he has paid out for such purpose is cost, irrespective of whether it is paid for the use of land or for any human services, and it must be very strange for him to be confronted with the distinctions which economic theory has been accustomed to uphold between costs that are costs and costs that are not.

Under the influence of the needs of an artificial theory, economists have, as we see, attributed an importance to the Differential Principle out of all proportion to its natural subordinate place. The same is the case with the Principle of Substitution, which has been placed in the foreground in an equally unwarranted manner. The student has got the impression that a price is paid for a thing because it could be substituted by another thing, and thereby a veil has been drawn over the fundamental fact that a price is paid primarily because of the scarcity of the thing. This is particularly conspicuous in the theory of interest. From the time of Jevons it has been customary to represent interest as a price that is paid because the use of capital can be substituted for labour. When it is said that interest is determined by the marginal productiveness of this substitution or, what comes to the same thing, by the "marginal productivity of the last extension of the period of production," and when such formulas are given out to represent the great solution of the puzzle of interest, then it is really time to react. It is all very well that the possibility of a substitution may have a modifying influence on the demand for the two factors of production in question, and therefore on their prices as well. But this fact is in no way essential to the existence of interest. Even if no substitution could take place, interest would have to be paid on account of the scarcity of the factor of production, called disposition over capital, in relation to the demand for it. It is the primary duty of the theory of interest to clear up this ground for the existence of interest. The same holds true in other cases where the Principle of Substitution has unduly been placed in the foreground. Of course, we should not neglect the influence of this principle. But in the whole theory of prices the Principle of Scarcity has to be recognized as the fundamental principle, and the other principles, required to make the problem determinable, have to be brought back to their right place as supplementary principles. This is what I have tried to do systematically in my *Theory of Social Economy.*

To this end the system of equations here described has proved to be of the highest value. Indeed, the true importance of the introduction of this system into the theory of prices can never be realized until it is understood that this choice of method necessarily leads up to the consequences which I have now outlined. There is nothing particularly remarkable in the fact that systems of equations are used in economics just as in other sciences, nor does the mere mention of them necessarily indicate a deeper insight into the central problems of economic theory. The whole bearing of the system of price equations is grasped only when it is looked upon as an expression for the uniform rôle which the Principle of Scarcity plays throughout the whole process of price-settlement and for the fundamentally symmetrical position of the different elementary factors of production within this process. It must also be recognized that the universal conception of cost which I have tried to expound here is intimately connected with the representation of the price-problem in the form of a system of equations. In these respects I fear much unclearness and much traditional doctrinairism have still to be removed before we can speak of the application of simultaneous equations to the price-problem as a definite achievement of economic science.

## CHAPTER IV

### The Scarcity Theory of Money

The place of the theory of money in the general economic theory is, according to what I have said, determined by the nature of the solution of the general problem of price-setting outlined in these lectures. We have postulated a monetary unit in which we can reckon all prices, and we have found that prices reckoned in this unit are determined by our system of equations except for a multiplicative factor. This degree of undeterminedness can only be removed by fixing the unit in which prices are reckoned. To show how this is done is the task of the theory of money.

In the historical development of money the need for a unit of reckoning and the need for a means of exchange stand out as two separate needs which may be satisfied by different means. The unit of reckoning always tends to become an abstract unit, the value of which is determined by the limitation of the supply of the means of payment which are recognized as valid for payments in that unit. This historical development which I have sketched in my second lecture shows the way in which the theory of money has to proceed. The theory has to study how and by what measures the supply of means of payment is regulated in different systems of money, and how the degree of scarcity thereby attained for this supply determines the purchasing power of the unit. This is the essence of the whole theory of money.

Thus we find that our treatment of the general economic theory not only gives to the theory of money its natural place as an integral part of the wider theory, but also in the main fixes the task and the methods of the theory of money.

If certain means of payment are recognized as valid for payments in an abstract unit, it is obvious that these means must be supplied in a certain scarcity in order that the unit may represent a definite value. For if means of payment could be had in any amount, any price could be paid and the unit of money would have no definite purchasing power. Thus the purchasing power of money is from the very outset necessarily connected with the scarcity of the supply of means of payment. The specific character of this connection must be made the subject of a closer investigation. What precise influence the supply of means of payment has on the purchasing power of the unit is a question which can, of course, be discussed theoretically, but which can hardly be answered definitely except by experience. The theory of money must, therefore, always have recourse to statistical material collected with a view to throwing light upon the connection between the general level of prices and the supply of means of payment.

There are many different ways of limiting the supply of means of payment, and the various forms of money are essentially characterized by these ways.

Theoretically, the simplest form of money is the paper money directly regulated by the State. If such a system of money is to possess definite stability, the State must fix the amount of paper money to be issued either at an absolute figure or per head, or better in a certain connection with general economic progress.

The essential thing is that the means of payment should exist at any given moment in a definite amount, and that this amount should be determined by State regulation. A more liberal supply of the means of payment will obviously cause the prices to rise. This is just the dangerous element in State-regulated paper money. For, in order to procure means for their expenses, Governments may issue more paper money, and thereby create a fresh purchasing power. As, however, this purchasing power is not balanced by a corresponding increase of commodities that can be bought, prices are bound to rise. We call this process inflation, and inflation in this case appears in its simplest and most distinct form.

The next form of money which the theory has to consider is the paper money controlled by a central bank. The supply of means of payment is now regulated in an essentially different manner. The bank does not create money in order to meet its own expenses, but hands over its notes to the public in the form of loans and discounts. The total amount of these advances is not fixed by the bank at a certain figure. In fact, it is left to the public to decide how much it wishes to borrow, and the bank has no other means of regulating the total supply than the conditions which it applies in advancing money. These conditions, therefore, determine the scarcity of the supply of means of payment. The bank can use several such conditions. In fact, a central bank always regulates more or less strictly the kind of "eligible securities" on which it is prepared to lend. It generally limits very sharply the period of its advances. It may even restrict the purposes for which advances are given, and so on. But all these means are only smaller means of second-rate importance. The essential means by which the supply of the means of payment of the bank is regulated is the price which the borrowers have to pay for their loans, i.e., the different rates of interest applied by the bank. These rates are generally determined by the most important of them, the minimum rate of discount or, as it is often called, the official bank rate. Thus it is clear that in the present case the supply of means of payment, and therefore also the purchasing power of the unit of money, is regulated essentially by the bank rate. This important result is, as we see, an immedi-

ate outcome of the form which we have given
to the central problem of the theory of money.
The validity of the thesis is sometimes denied,
and it is contended that the central bank has
not the power of exercising such an influence.
People who hold this view, however, are bound
to answer the question: How, then, in our case
are the supply of means of payment and the
purchasing power of money determined? If
they were to take this question seriously into
consideration, they would soon discover that
there is, in fact, no other answer than that
given here.

The question of how an increase in the bank
rate affects the supply of means of payment
and the purchasing power of money has been,
and still is, the subject of very much discussion,
and I have, therefore, in my writings given
much attention to the clearing up of this question. The general theory of prices shows that
there is always a certain rate of interest necessary in order to maintain the capital market in
equilibrium, i.e., to create a balance between
the supply and demand of disposition over capital. Now, the first thing we should ask of a
rational bank policy is that it should under no

circumstances disturb this balance. The banks should lend to the public, over and above their own means, only what they can borrow from the public. Thus the banks should not use their capacity for creating a nominal purchasing power in the form of their own means of payment in order to satisfy a demand for capital which cannot be satisfied by actual savings. In order to avoid this fault, the banks must obviously keep their rates at a height corresponding to those rates of interest which would keep the capital market in equilibrium. This rule particularly applies to the central bank. If the bank rate is kept lower than what corresponds to the real scarcity of the capital market, demands for capital will be directed to the central bank, and will, to a certain extent, be satisfied by the creation of a surplus of means of payment. This means inflation. On the other hand, if the bank rate is kept higher than the capital market would require, means of payment are paid back to the central bank, and a process of deflation takes place.

The rule that the bank rate should correspond to the interest rate of the capital market can, however, not be applied directly, simply because we do not know the rate of interest which would keep the capital market in equilibrium. The banks have no other way of ascertaining the correctness of their policy than by observing the effect of the bank rate: if the general level of prices rises, this proves that the bank rate is too low. The bank rate, therefore, must be kept so high that the general level of prices remains practically constant. The task is, however, a difficult one, because the bank should not wait to take action until the rise of prices has already taken place, but should rather by its discount policy prevent any rise.

Opinions differ very much with regard to the effect of the bank rate on prices. Among practical business men it even seems to be a prevalent idea that a raising of the bank rate must increase the costs of production, and therefore generally enhance prices. Even theorists are not always quite clear about this point. In the light of the general theory which I have now outlined the question becomes very simple. As long as the bank rate coincides with the equilibrium rate of interest of the capital market, it has no effect on the general level of prices, which then may remain constant. It is, in this connection, quite irrelevant whether the rate of interest is high or low. If, again, the bank rate is above the rate of the capital market, a fall in the general price-level will follow. But then this fall is caused exclusively by the difference between the rates, and has nothing to do with their absolute levels. A high rate of interest on the capital market has always, of course, as I have shown in my previous lectures, an influence on the relative prices of commodities, the prices of those commodities being raised relatively for the production of which particularly much disposition over capital is required. But then, instead, other prices must fall to such an extent that the general level of prices remains unaltered. A rise or fall in this general level can be caused by the bank rate only by its being kept lower or higher than what corresponds to an equilibrium of the capital market.

The third case which the theory of money has to consider is the case of a pure gold currency. This case is rather theoretical, because such a currency does not exist. But still it is worth considering in order to clear the ground for the treatment of our actual gold standards. Supposing, then, that there are no other means of payment than gold coins, and that the public has a free right to have gold minted as well as to smelt down gold coins, and that, in addition, gold imports and exports are unhampered, we find that the total supply of means of payment is not determined as an independent quantity, but is closely connected with the total stock of gold in the country or in the world at large. For, according to our assumption, gold can freely move to and from the stock of money of the country. Nevertheless, there is a certain scarcity in the supply of means of payment. This scarcity is closely connected with the general scarcity of the supply of gold, and is, to a certain extent, dependent upon the demand for gold for other than monetary purposes and from other countries. Although, therefore, the scarcity is not fixed by a definite figure, it is nevertheless an objective fact determining the value of the monetary unit. In such a gold standard, therefore, the country has once and for all given up exercising any influence on the purchasing power of its money and bound up this purchasing power with that of gold.

On the other hand, gold is not the money of the country. The unit is not, as is very often believed, a certain weight of gold, but has, even in the case of this pure gold standard, an independent existence as an abstract unit. This is clear from the fact that the price of gold can vary about a theoretical par within the limits determined by the cost of minting on the one side, and by the cost of smelting on the other, or, better, by the minimum weight of gold contained in a certain sum of actual coins. Indeed, the rules of the mint law relating to these details, which in the old view formed the essence of the whole system of money, are seen in the light of the present theory to represent mere technical means for securing that the price of gold shall be fixed within certain narrow limits. By this fixing of the price of gold a definite value is given to the abstract unit of money.

After these preliminaries we are ready to take up the discussion of the most important system of money, the gold standard with a paper circulation. From the beginning of my economic work I have chosen to regard this system of money as a paper standard regulated by a central bank with the object of keeping the monetary unit in a certain parity with gold. This view, which is an immediate logical consequence of our general conception of money, doubtless reflects also in the most natural way what really takes place in the administration of a modern gold standard. Without doubt, in such a standard, we have to do with an abstract unit of money whose purchasing power is determined by the supply of the means of payment created by the banks. This supply is, as in the case of a stable paper standard, regulated essentially by means of the bank rate. The task of the banks is then to uphold such a scarcity in this supply that the unit can be kept approximately at par with gold. This is the same as to say that the supply of means of payment should be regulated so that the price of gold will be approximately the same as the theoretical price indicated by the mint law. An exact equality can never be maintained. In a gold standard with a paper circulation the price of gold is continually varying within narrow limits about its par. This fact which is quite familiar to banking people is very often overlooked in theoretical discussions. It is, as I observed in the case of the pure gold standard, theoretically of essential importance, because it shows that the unit is not a certain weight of gold, in which case a variation of the price of gold would be logically impossible, but is, as always, an abstract unit, the value of which is determined exclusively by the supply of the means of payment valid in that unit. It is interesting to observe here what predominance the latest development of monetary policy has given to this view of the essential nature of the gold standard. In fact, Mr. Churchill's gold standard, where the circulation of gold coins is abolished, stands out for everybody in full daylight as a paper standard guaranteed to be kept in a certain parity with gold by the provisions which oblige the central bank to buy and sell gold at fixed prices. Thus by the new British legislation the real essence of the gold standard is brought to the fore, and the technical details of the mint law, to which the old-fashioned textbook gave such disproportionate prominence, but which were after all only subordinate means, are definitely thrown on the scrap-heap.

By our method a fundamental unity is secured for the treatment of all kinds of monetary standards. We see that in all cases the purchasing power of money depends exclusively on the limitation of the supply of the means of payment. Whenever such means are supplied by a central bank, we must conclude that the purchasing power of the unit of money is regulated by the credit policy of that bank, and particularly by the rates of interest which it applies; or that, as I have formulated it already in *The Nature and Necessity of Interest,* "all schemes for securing stability, though they differ considerably in the means they propose to use, ultimately depend on the same expedient—a wise administration of the bank rate."[1]

This result has shown itself to be of value for a clear judgment of one of the most important and most urgent economic questions of our own time, viz., the question of the restoration of the gold standard after the long period of violently inflated paper standards. Many people seem to believe that there are almost mystical difficulties involved in this restoration of the gold standard. It has also been said that the gold standard is a standard only for rich nations with well-balanced finances! It is then

[1] P. 163.

very useful to state that the gold standard is at bottom nothing else than a paper standard where the supply of means of payment is limited to such a scarcity as will keep the price of gold approximately constant. From this point of view it is immediately clear that the first step in our work of restoration must be the stabilization of the present paper standards of the different countries. It is then also a very natural conclusion, to which I have endeavoured to give the greatest weight as a piece of practical advice, that this stabilization, in order to be achieved with the least possible delay and without unnecessary fresh disturbances, should generally take place in the neighbourhood of the actual present value of the currency. Only in such cases where this value was very near to the pre-war value could the restoration of that pre-war value be looked upon as practical policy. It was obvious that in all cases the currency could be restored to the gold standard as soon as the stabilization had been carried out. For we had then only to fix legally the gold par which had actually been attained. The difficulties of maintaining such a gold standard and the means for doing it are seen, in the light of the theory here presented, to be essentially the same as in the case of a stabilized paper standard. Therefore the transition from the regulated paper standard to the gold standard is no very marvellous or very dangerous step. It must, however, be observed that, in the event of the value of gold itself in relation to commodities in general showing considerable variations, the introduction of the gold standard will bring about the extra difficulty that the value of the money unit in relation to commodities can no longer be kept constant, but must be adapted to that of gold. Of course, this is a drawback of the gold standard, but it is inherent in the system, and when we nevertheless accept the gold standard as the solution of the monetary problem, it is because we prefer making our standard dependent upon an outside objective factor, such as the value of gold, rather than leaving it to the caprices of politics.

The general theory of money which I have now sketched forms the ultimate theoretical basis for all that I have written on the subject of money during and after the War. It underlies my Memoranda to the League of Nations on *The World's Monetary Problem*, as well as my work *Money and Foreign Exchange After 1914*, and has a particular bearing on my latest book on *The Problem of Stabilization*, which, owing to lack of time, I have unfortunately only been able to publish in Swedish.

If, according to what has now been said, our actual gold standards are paper standards regulated to correspond to the value of gold, the question remains how the value of gold itself is determined. There can be no other answer to this question than that the value of gold is determined by the scarcity of the world's total supply of gold in comparison with the world's total demand. However, the supply of gold to be taken into consideration cannot be confined to the stock of a single country, nor, as is often assumed, to the world's monetary stock of gold. Neither of these quantities has an independent existence. In a gold standard, gold is free to move between countries as well as between the monetary and the industrial stock of gold. This mobility of gold is a fundamental characteristic of the gold standard. We have, therefore, necessarily to find out how the general level of prices in a gold standard depends on the world's total supply of gold. I have made such an investigation, of which the first results were published in Swedish in 1904, and which has since been extended. The whole material with diagrams is contained in my *Theory of Social Economy,* and I shall here only try to give a general idea of my method of procedure.

The economic progress of the world must, of course, make an increased supply of gold necessary if the value of gold shall be invariable, i.e., if the general level of prices of commodities shall be constant. We cannot therefore speak of a superfluity or a scarcity of gold in any period without referring these conceptions to a supply which can be regarded as normal for the period. But what supply is normal? That is the same as to ask: What rate of increase in the world's gold supply has been necessary during a certain period to enable the general level of prices to remain constant during that period? Of course, this question can only be answered by experience, i.e., by collecting statistical material for a lengthy period. To this end, the period from 1850 to 1910 is particularly convenient, because the general level of gold prices in 1910 was practically the same as in 1850. In this period, however, the world's total stock of gold was multiplied by the figure 5.2, which corresponds to an annual increase of 2.8 per cent. If, therefore, the world's stock of gold had increased uniformly during the whole period by 2.8 per cent every year, the stock in 1910 would have been precisely what it actually was, and there would have been no reason why the supply of gold should have caused any variation in the general level of prices in the meantime. Such a uniform growth of the world's stock of gold from 1850 to 1910, therefore, may be taken to represent the world's normal gold supply for every year in the period. The actual gold stock of the world was sometimes greater, sometimes smaller, and we are in a position to give in precise figures a measure of the superfluity or scarcity of gold at any time of the period under consideration. For this purpose I have introduced the conception of a *relative gold supply,* which is for any given year the actual gold supply divided by the normal gold supply.

This relative gold supply is the only factor which can reasonably be assumed to have any influence on the general level of prices. The object of our investigation must, therefore, be to find out how far the actual variations of the general level of gold prices during the period from 1850 to 1910 are explained by corresponding variations in the relative gold supply. Thus we have to compare two curves of which one represents the relative gold supply and the other the general level of gold prices. It is then immediately proved that the latter curve contains sharp short-time fluctuations which have no counterpart at all in the very even curve representing the relative gold supply. These price fluctuations are easily recognized as connected with periods of prosperity and depression. We can immediately draw the conclusion that trade cycles have nothing to do with the supply of gold. Eliminating the corresponding short-time price fluctuations from the curve representing the general level of prices, we find a curve which corresponds to our curve of relative gold supply in a most striking manner. The conclusion is that the long-time variations of the general level of prices essentially depend upon variations in the relative gold supply.

In this investigation nothing has been said about the possible influence of variations in the demand for gold. A closer examination of our curve shows that the demand for gold has on two occasions only been able to exercise any influence on the general price-level. The most important of these occasions was the enormous American demand for gold during the period when the gold standard had to be restored after the Civil War inflation period. With the said exceptions, the demand for gold shows itself to have been a rather passive factor in the formation of the world's gold prices.

The results of my investigations in this matter may be said to give the final answer to the much disputed question of the validity of the quantitative theory of money, as far as the dependence of the general level of prices on the supply of gold is concerned.

If the world's total stock of gold is to increase by 2.8 per cent per annum, the annual production must not only correspond to that factor, but must also make up for the year's definite loss of gold, which may be taken on an average to represent 0.2 per cent of the total stock. Thus the annual production must amount to 3 per cent of the total stock at the beginning of every year. Economic textbooks

have always taught us that the remarkable stability of the value of gold—a stability which
makes gold particularly serviceable as a monetary standard—depends on the fact that the
world had accumulated such an enormous stock
of gold that the annual production was neg-
ligible in comparison with the accumulated
stock. This doctrine, which has been so universally accepted without any criticism, proves,
in the light of our figures, to be entirely futile.
Stability requires, not that the accumulated
stock of gold should be "enormous," or anything like that, in comparison with the annual
production, but simply that it should be 33⅓
times as large.

As the annual supply required for stability
is a certain percentage of the stock accumulated, it must obviously grow at the same rate
as the stock itself. This is a very important
conclusion. The consequence, indeed, is that,
if the production of gold, however abundant it
may be at the present moment, should remain
constant, it must become insufficient within a
certain number of years. For the production
increases the stock, and when the stock grows,
the annual increase of the stock which corre-

sponds to the economic progress of the world must grow likewise, and sooner or later outgrow the constant production. If the annual production of gold falls short of the percentage of the accumulated stock required to meet economic progress, the general level of prices in a gold standard is bound to fall. If, therefore, the world should be confronted with the impossibility of increasing the annual gold production, and consequently with the necessity of being satisfied with a constant gold production —not to speak of the case of an actually diminishing production—the world would have to face a continual and incessant fall of the general level of prices with a consequent economic depression. Thus the gold standard must be said to be a satisfactory standard only on the condition that the world is able to increase indefinitely its annual production of gold at the same rate as characterizes the world's general economic progress.

In the present situation these observations have a particular interest. For the world's annual production of gold has now gone back considerably from the maximum amount reached in 1915, and is now much less than 3 per cent of the accumulated stock of gold. This, however, must mean for the future a scarcity in the supply of gold, and therefore a fall in the general level of prices. Such a scarcity is inevitable unless new gold discoveries of a quite startling character should alter the whole situation. For the moment, however, this trouble is thrust aside by the temporary superfluity of gold, caused by the monetary incidents of the War and the first post-war period. In fact, we have here to deal with a violent reduction in the demand for gold, unique of its kind in the whole history of money. Gold has been expelled from a number of European countries, and, to a great extent, has accumulated in the United States, where a great superfluity of gold has been caused thereby. The consequence has been an extraordinary rise in the general level of gold prices. Indeed, the rise of prices would have been still greater if the Americans had not found it advisable to handle their gold stock to a great extent as if it were a reserve for future needs. People have been so much impressed by this superfluity of gold that they have, in most cases, been unable to take a broad view of the situation. But the superfluity is only a temporary phenomenon. Continental Europe will require gold for the restoration of the gold standard, and thus gold is bound to find its way back again to Europe. In fact, this movement has already begun, and the superfluity of gold which has caused so much unnecessary fear in the last few years is already beginning to disappear. The most important thing in this connection, however, is the future progress of the world. This progress will perhaps be somewhat slower than it was in the period 1850-1910, but the world is certainly not going to acquiesce in a state of stagnation. The present production will, therefore, necessarily prove insufficient. If it is impossible very materially to increase the production of gold, the world will have to face a serious scarcity of gold as soon as the part of the American gold stock, which can now be regarded as kept in reserve, has been absorbed by the world's growing needs.

Under these circumstances a clear-sighted monetary policy is bound earnestly to consider the question whether it would not be possible to restrict the world's monetary demand for gold to such an extent as to prevent the coming scarcity from exercising a depressing influence on prices. The International Financial Conference held in Genoa in 1922 took up this question and made express recommendations for the limitation of the world's monetary demand for gold. These recommendations were made with a clear insight into the threatening danger of a scarcity of gold caused by the present production being kept about constant during a period when the progress of the world must be expected to require a steadily increasing annual supply of gold.

A theory of money which makes the scarcity of the supply of means of payment the basis for the explanation of how the value of money is determined, and which regards the gold standards of the various countries simply as paper standards regulated to be kept in a certain parity with gold—such a theory was obviously particularly well suited to aid in forming a clear judgment as to what was really going on in the monetary sphere during the War. The continual creation of fresh currency which in all countries was defended on the ground of the extraordinary needs of the situation—and even on the ground of the rise in prices!—could be immediately recognized, in the light of this theory, as a creation of nominal purchasing power inevitably bound to compete with the legitimate purchasing power already existing, and thus to cause prices to rise. A long struggle, however, had to be engaged in before this simple truth was generally acknowledged. It is still doubtful whether it would ever have become so universally accepted as it now is, had not scientific teaching gained immensely powerful support from the lesson of the catastrophic destruction of currencies in which inflation had been carried on in astronomical dimensions.

I have never been able to recognize the so-called quantitative theory of money as a doctrine the truth of which must be acknowledged a priori. It has always seemed to me that the effect of an increased supply of means of payment on the purchasing power of money must be studied in the light of actual experience. With regard to the supply of gold, I have carried out such a study along the lines I have just described. For the examination of the theoretically most simple case of the pure paper standard, the War and post-war years were to contribute material of the most overwhelming abundance and diversity. For the advancement of economic science this was a unique opportunity. My investigations led me to express the quantitative theory in a form which seemed better to correspond to what actually happened than earlier formulas did. My formulation is as follows: If fresh means of payment are created—whether in the form of legal tender currency or in the form of banking means of payment—additional purchasing power is created. The result must be a rise in prices. We cannot say exactly how great this rise will be. But once a rise in prices having taken place, the genuine need for means of payment will obviously increase in the same proportion. Thus the public will keep so much of the fresh means of payment as it wants at the higher price-level. The rest of the freshly created means of payment will flow back to the banks which have created them. The result is that the general level of prices and the total supply of means of payment have both increased in the same proportion. Now, if this process is repeated incessantly, we shall find the supply of means of payment rise continually, and at the same time the general level of prices rise in about the same proportion. The cause of this simultaneous and proportional rise of both factors is, without doubt, the continual creation of artificial purchasing power in the form of fresh means of payment. This determination of what is cause and effect in the process is the most important side of the quantitative theory of money, which in the form now given seems to be unobjectionable. But as this fixation of cause laid the responsibility for inflation where it should lie, the most strenuous efforts were made on the part of the authorities in different countries to prove the incorrectness of my analysis and to hide the real connection behind masses of obscure phrases. In this struggle disproportional importance was attributed to all deviations from the theory which actual experience could possibly discover. But those who laid most stress on these deviations were usually unable to give any consistent explanation whatever of the corresponding occurrences. This is natural enough. For such deviations as, e.g., a rise in prices over and above the increase in the supply of means of payment can without doubt be best studied for what they are, viz., deviations from a general rule which has the undeniable value that it represents the essential part of the movements in question.

For a true understanding of the extraordinary disturbances in the exchanges which followed upon inflation, my earlier theoretical investigations also proved to be a great help. In my university lectures I had been accustomed to build up the theory of exchanges on the fundamental fact that what we pay for a foreign currency must be determined essentially by what we get for that currency when we wish to buy something for it, i.e., by its internal purchasing power. We must, therefore, pay for a foreign currency a price which is in inverse proportion to the general level of prices in the foreign country. It is equally clear that what we can pay in our own currency must be in direct proportion to the general level of prices in our own country. Thus the rate of exchange must be determined essentially by the quotient of the internal purchasing powers of the two currencies concerned.

This theory refers primarily to paper currencies. But as gold currencies are regarded essentially as paper currencies regulated to keep the value of gold at a theoretical par, but practically within the gold points, the theory applies likewise to gold standards so long as exchanges remain within the gold points. The possibility of gold payments is a factor modifying the movements of the exchange, preventing it from passing the gold points as long as any gold is available for the purpose. In this way it had been possible to construct a theory of exchanges with a uniform validity for all monetary standards. Obviously this proved of great advantage for forming a correct judgment of the extraordinary alterations which took place in the world's exchanges during the period of inflation.

In the beginning of the revolution of exchanges all sorts of devices were resorted to in order to explain, or perhaps rather to excuse, movements of exchanges which were felt to be discreditable. It was generally held that the disturbances were of a quite temporary character, and that they would correct themselves as soon as the world's trade should be restored to normal conditions. In opposition to these views a scientific analysis showed that the essential cause of the alterations of the exchanges was to be found in alterations in the internal values of the currencies, i.e., in their internal purchasing powers. These alterations could only have the effect of altering the real parity between the currencies. The new equilibrium of the exchanges must be determined by the product of the old parity and the quotient of the degrees of inflation of both currencies. For this new par I introduced the name, "the purchasing power parity." Of course, the old parity was just as much a purchasing power parity, and the new parity had developed from that only by alterations of the internal purchasing power of the two currencies concerned.

It is hardly possible to calculate exactly the purchasing power parity between two currencies exclusively on the ground of our knowledge of prices in both countries. There are too many factors involved in the problem making it too complicated for direct calculation. But if we once know a parity which has existed in a state of equilibrium at certain levels of prices in the two countries, we may take this parity as a starting-point for the calculation of a parity at other price-levels. This is just what I have done in calculating the purchasing power parity of the War and post-war period on the basis of the actual pre-war parity. Of course, there was much criticism against my methods and my results. But the critics were divided into two parties, of which one thought my doctrine absurd and the other called it a truism. Gradually, however, sufficient experience has been gathered to show the essential correctness of the theory of the purchasing power parity and of the practical usefulness of this theory for forming a judgment of the true values of exchanges which were subjected to violent market fluctuations. In this case, as in all other cases where an economic theory is involved, deviations existed, and antagonists of the theory, or of any definite theory whatsoever, tried to make the most of these deviations. In fact, the deviations were sometimes important and revealed very interesting phenomena. But these phenomena could best be studied if the main cause of the alteration of the exchange, viz., the alteration of the purchasing power parity, had first been taken into account. I have devoted much attention to the deviations of the exchanges from the purchasing power parities, to their causes and to their effects, particularly on international trade, and now, when the conception of the purchasing power parity has become practically universally accepted, such investigations are carried on in all parts of the world. It may be hoped that in this way our understanding of the problem of exchanges will be greatly advanced.

The final proof of the validity of the theory of the purchasing power parities could not, of course, be given before normal conditions had begun to be restored, with the result that the deviations from the purchasing power parity could be expected to disappear. This has in the main been the case, for some few years, with the most important of the world's currencies, the pound sterling and the dollar. Since 1919 the actual exchange between these currencies, as I have shown in the recent *Quarterly Report of the Skandinaviska Kreditaktiebolaget*,[1] has been very nearly determined by their purchasing power parity. The mean of the rates of exchange for the whole period is almost exactly in accordance with this parity.

[1] Stockholm, April 1925.

The only deviations of importance which occur are caused by the movements of capital between the countries. But these movements should, at least as far as they are caused by a difference in the rates of interest in the two countries, naturally be taken into account by the general theory of purchasing power parity, and cannot therefore properly be spoken of as exceptions from this theory.

.    .    .    .    .    .    .

I have now come to the end of this short analysis of my economic work. But this analysis would be very incomplete indeed if I did not add to it my most hearty acknowledgment of the great indebtedness in which I stand to English economic thinking for all it has taught me both as regards clearness of reasoning and as regards the close connection between economic theory and the practical problems of economic life. In this indebtedness should be included also an indebtedness for the very useful lessons I have learnt from the unrivalled virtues of British banking and finance. Finally, I have to add my thanks to all my personal friends in England in the scientific world as well as in the sphere of business. The moral and intellectual support which I have had from these personal connections has been for me, for more than a quarter of a century, of incalculable value in working out my fundamental thoughts on economics.